# SCOTLAND

## THE CASE FOR OPTIMISM

# SCOTLAND

## THE CASE FOR OPTIMISM

by

JIM SILLARS

POLYGON
EDINBURGH

First published in 1986 by Polygon,
48 Pleasance, Edinburgh EH8 9TJ

Typeset by EUSPB,
48 Pleasance, Edinburgh EH8 9TJ


ISBN 0 948275 16 2


Printed and bound by Bell and Bain Ltd., Glasgow.

To
MARGO
with love, respect and admiration for
all she has done for Scotland.

# CONTENTS

## *Part 1:*
## THE TRAVELS OF A
## LATE DEVELOPER

## *Part 2:*
## SCOTTISH THEMES

# INTRODUCTION

AS I WRITE in late October 1985, even Scottish Conservatives are becoming alarmed by the threats to Scotland's place as an industrial nation. The British Steel Corporation's decision to close the Gartcosh steel rolling mill, thus leaving the Ravenscraig steel works vulnerable to future closure, has given an electrifying shock to the Scottish body politic. With the exception of a few of Mrs Thatcher's placemen in the Scottish Conservative Party organisation, the whole community is deeply disturbed. About time too. From 1979 to the present day has been a calamitous period in Scottish history. We have endured the total shutdown of the Linwood car plant, closure of coal mines, steel and shipbuilding redundancies, the loss of the Fort William pulp mill, the loss of British Leyland as a viable concern at Bathgate and closure of the aluminium smelter at Invergordon. These have been hammer blows at main pillars of Scottish economic life.

When one compares the present gloom with the vibrant scene of ten years ago, it is scarcely believable that we are looking at the same people, the same nation. Then, we stood full of vigour and confidence, poised to enter a new age wherein all challenges and problems seemed capable of solution. Today, ours is a fearful, anxious, nail-biting nation ruminating on Burns's salutation to human despair, "An' forward tho' I canna see, I guess and fear".

How have we come to this pass? This book is an attempt to provide a partial answer and to show a way forward. By rights it should not be a book from my pen alone. The idea was conceived by Stephen Maxwell. It was to have been a joint effort, with the first part devoted to two separate autobiographical pieces. We would seek to identify major influences on

1

our personal political development and that of Scotland as a whole. Two very different people, from different class backgrounds, telling separate stories about how they both came to share the same position by the time Scotland entered the 1980s. Stephen believed this approach would be of more interest to the general reader than a simple restatement of our views on recent political history. It is after all human beings who stand central to developments. Human intangibles such as hope, revulsion, anger, optimism, fear, spirit and will which do so much to shape our lives as a community. The second part was to consist of a series of essays on individual issues.

Marriage, a new family, and job changes made it impossible for Stephen to complete his contribution. I have been encouraged by him and others to publish the work I managed to undertake. I have stuck to Stephen's formula.

I would also like to acknowledge the encouragement and assistance given to me by Bob Brown, Alex Neil, Alex Salmond, Kenny MacAskill, Grant Baird and Donald Rutherford who had the thankless task of guiding and editing the project, and did so with good humour and much patience. Above all, I would like to place on record my debt to my wife Margo MacDonald and four children, Matthew and Julie Sillars and Petra and Zoe MacDonald, and my daughter-in-law Jacqueline. Without their prompting and encouragement I would never have started and once started would never have finished.

I trust those interested in Scottish politics will accept my word that while I obviously consulted Margo about the issues to be covered, and discussed with her many of the events of the past ten years, what is said herein are entirely my views. Although married, we hold firmly to our independent views on politics and our interpretation of events, and in political issues speak only for ourselves. Any one person can give only a partial view of events and I claim no more than that. I do believe that my wife's views on things past and things to come would be of value to Scottish political life. Perhaps we shall all be lucky enough to have them from her in due course.

*Part 1:*

# THE TRAVELS OF A
# LATE DEVELOPER

# Chapter 1

# PREPARATION FOR PARLIAMENT

THESE CHAPTERS ARE autobiographical in style but not an autobiography. I am not trying to rise above my natural station. One fate that must be avoided is to fall at the famous Scottish hurdle of: "Him! I kent his faither."

I start with my faither, Matthew Sillars, now a retired British Rail engine driver. He was one of a long line of Sillars who found employment on the railways. I start with my father because he anchored my beliefs to the Labour Party. Although I proved to be a late developer, not joining the Labour Party until twenty-three years of age, three incidents in my early days, all revolving round my father, had a decisive influence on all my political development.

First, there was the 1945 general election. Do not misunderstand. I was then eight years old and not even aware that an election was on. What the war's end meant for me was the certainty of seeing, for the first time, senior football played at Somerset Park, the home of Ayr United. I was football daft: kicking a tanner ba' all the way to school, around the playground and all the way back home again. I played headers and keepie-uppie until I was hauled into bed, there to dream of reaching the age of twelve and thus qualify for selection for the school team, Newton Park.

The election campaign passed me by, but there was no way I could avoid knowing about the result. We were listening to the wireless when my father's whole being radiated sheer joy. One moment he was standing around tense and anxious, the next he

5

was a man possessed, rushing downstairs and outside shouting "We've won, we've won", to hug and dance Mrs Logan, a miner's wife who lived across the garden path from us. My mother just beamed at everybody. To my persistent questions afterwards, my father gave the clear impression that a great good had conquered a great evil and that the "Labour Government", a phrase my father repeated like an incantation, would really look after the working-class folk. I believed him without question.

Next, there was the 1951 general election when Churchill was returned to power. The atmosphere in our house was funereal, with my father shaking his head time and time again, telling my mother in an agonised voice, "They'll make us pay for this." So deep was his anguish, and so powerful his influence, that I honestly thought that everything in the world would change for the worst including the weather. Listening to the old man, I felt sure the sun would but rarely shine through the clouds again.

Of course, life for a young working-class boy, daft about football and crazy about golf, quickly went back to normal. The sun did shine, and life revolved around the fortunes of Ayr United's struggles to get into the First Division. After my father and grandfather, the most important person in my life was Norrie McNeil, the Ayr United centre half and captain. Week after week he played a stormer of a game. Even when my cousin Jim Clive, centre forward for Kilmarnock, came up against him in an Ayrshire derby I hoped Norrie would come out on top.

I lived from Saturday to Saturday. School was a prison sentence. Newton Park primary only became tolerable because I finally made the first team at football, as outside left. The secondary I attended later, Ayr Academy, played rugby not football and held no attractions whatever. I flunked frequently and didn't even bother to attend in the final three months. I had a love for books, which came from the promptings of my grandfather, but the books were picked at random. One time it might be a cowboy story, or a book about earthquakes, or ancient Egypt. I read Greek mythology, *All Quiet on the Western Front*, and *Pilgrim's Progress*. The latter was the only prize I ever won at school, for Bible studies. I remember struggling through it from cover to cover, thinking it was just a boy's adventure story. The people donating the prize would have been disappointed to learn that it was not until many years later I realised that *Pilgrim's Progress* had any religious significance.

So, life went on its normal way. As a railway engine driver my father had a reasonable income by working-class standards. That meant that we were not poor, but were far from well off. Those were the post-war austerity years and life was at the level of bare necessities, with cheap seats at the local cinema filling the need for entertainment. Our holidays consisted of using my father's free rail tickets to visit my mother's relatives in Dundee, where we all packed into a room and kitchen, sleeping three to a bed. I never knew what it was to have a meal in a restaurant. The time I hated most was the Glasgow Fair, when we let our bedroom to strangers. The time I liked most was during the Ayr race meeting in September, when Codona's Fair pitched themselves only a few hundred yards from our house. If my father had managed to pick the winner of the Ayr Gold Cup, which he often did, his generosity knew no bounds and it was a magic time for my brother, my young sister and me.

That was the background against which we grew up. By 1949 my big brother Bob had become an apprentice bricklayer, which was a source of great satisfaction in the family. Becoming a tradesman was important, so important in fact that it was something widely discussed in the school playground and on the way to the football on a Saturday afternoon. The reason was that getting a trade was a precondition of going to Canada. Going to Canada, or Australia, or Rhodesia was an accepted fact of life in our society. If you wanted to get on in life, then it was best to get out of Scotland.

In January 1953, I followed Bob into the building trade. I was fifteen and became an apprentice plasterer. It was the wrong choice and within a year I moved on to my real love, the railway. From my great-grandfather down to my father (including a number of relatives) we had been a railway family.

This move eventually led to the third incident in which my father was to shape and form my outlook politically and industrially.

It arose out of the railway strike in the summer of 1955, when ASLEF withdrew their labour. My father was a member of ASLEF, a craft union for locomotive footplatemen. The other main rail union was the NUR, but it was a general union with a minority of drivers and firemen in membership. I joined ASLEF at the age of sixteen during my first weeks of employment, but then no one came to collect our dues. Later I joined the NUR. This was because of the influence of my grandfather. He had been an engine driver, but he firmly believed in the unity of all railwaymen and profoundly disagreed with a separate union for drivers and firemen. I wasn't a keen trade unionist and never attended branch meetings. My priorities in those days were to identify the pubs which were not too fussy about a boy's age before serving up the drink.

ASLEF had been pressing for a wage increase and finally decided on strike action. My own union, the NUR, was not coming out. As a young cleaner/fireman I was earning "big" money. Cleaners in winter mainly did labouring work, such as clearing mountains of hot ashes dumped out of fireboxes of steam engines or filling hutches with coal and tipping them into the tenders of locomotives. In the summer time we became full-time firemen, acting as holiday relief crew. By comparison with building apprentices we earned good money, so my stake in the issues of the strike seemed non-existent. The driver with whom I was paired that summer was also in the NUR. We booked off from backshift on the Saturday night, with the strike due to start at midnight. My driver was emphatic about coming back to work on the Monday and advised me to do the same. It was an ASLEF decision to strike and we in the NUR were not consulted or involved.

When I woke at home on the Sunday morning, I found my father saw it differently. ASLEF was a craft union, whose members had a great sense of pride in their work. Most footplatemen loved their work, indeed it was their hobby. In our family, for example, it was a matter of deep satisfaction that my grandfather's engine No. 4647 (it was *his* not the railway company's) was subsequently driven by my father, and then had me on the footplate as fireman. That engine was a living thing for us: my grandfather asked for it, and he, my father and I would discuss its various parts and performance the way Lord Rosebery would no doubt discuss one of his racehorses.

In the view of ASLEF, the accumulated knowledge and ability of its members, the responsibility they took for the lives of hundreds of people on trains and the millions of tons of goods transported, merited special award in the railway pay scales. Whatever ASLEF won would also go to the NUR footplatemen. ASLEF tended to see their members as the cream of the railway.

On that first Sunday morning of the strike, I was adamant. I was not coming out and a major row ensued between me and my father with my mother begging me to listen. Finally, after a couple of hours of me digging in my heels, my father spoke with more eloquence and vehemence than I have heard before or since. He was on difficult ground on the question of ASLEF membership because many of the men he most admired in local politics, including the father of Willie Ross, had been footplate members of the NUR. Never once was he able to best my grandfather in the latter's advocoacy of unity under one union. I had thrown my grandfather's case in his face all morning. He abandoned the ASLEF versus NUR debate. Instead my father invoked the family's reputation in the context of a working-class struggle. We were well respected in the trade union railway circles. If I went to work, crossing the picket lines, the label of "blackleg" would be attached to me and mine. The result would be perpetual shame, a mark of Cain that could never be wiped away. I listened to all this and I remember my father asking me if I knew that a blackleg was the lowest of the low, a traitor to his class. It was inconceivable that a son of his could be a scab. He was right. Young as I was, put on the spot as a striker or a blackleg, I went on strike. It was many years later, in the Dam

Park Hall in Ayr in the miners' strike of 1972, that I was to witness Guy Stobbs, the Ayrshire miners' agent, quell a small revolt among young miners by the same blunt exposition of what the label "blackleg" meant.

The ASLEF strike was an education. I did my turn on picket duty and went to all the meetings and rallies. I saw and felt the bitterness boil up in men as, with the days passing without a break in the government or British Rail attitude, they grew desperate. That bitterness led to unsavoury incidents, such as the hounding of several NUR drivers and firemen who still remained at work. I felt a certain relief at not being on picket duty when these planned humiliations took place, but I understood that we were at war with the government, and that only a completely solid front would give us any chance of winning. Also, I was part of, and had the wit to register, the phenomenon that the more reluctant people are to engage in strike action, the harder their attitude becomes during that strike. In the end we were beaten, and I can still recall our march back to the railway sheds at night. Before we lined up outside the strike headquarters, our leaders told us that we had not lost our dignity. I grew up a good bit during that strike and marched along with my mates on my own with my father somewhere else in the crowd.

I doubt if anything could have altered the attitudes inherited from my father but that strike reinforced them. As part of the effort to maintain members' interest, morale and spirit, trade union leaders poured out the fruits of research on the unfair and immoral division of wealth and invoked the spirit of working-class solidarity and traditional working-class goals of a free and just society. It all left a lasting impression.

Shortly thereafter I became restless and sought wider horizons. I was almost tempted by a recruiting agent for the Rhodesian Railways but as a boy, listening to an exciting boxing commentary, I had been outraged when the black man, who knocked hell out of his white opponent, lost the verdict. The commentator talked about the "colour bar" as the reason. There was nothing noble or sophisticated about my reaction: I just thought the better man should always win whether he was black or white. When the recruiting agent told us that we would have black servants, he lost my interest and that of my mates. He got no one from the depot. Instead, in September 1955, one month before my eighteenth birthday, I joined the Royal Navy as a radio operator, looking forward to seeing the world as it was painted by the attractive naval recruiting propaganda of those years.

I joined at Portsmouth and had my first experience of culture shock. About a dozen of us landed there from the West of Scotland where we merged with larger groups from many parts of England. It was only when we tried to converse that I realised the huge difference between the language of everyday Lowland Scotland and most parts of England. I could understand them but they either could not or refused to understand me.

I endured one piece of horrific embarrassment when I visited my first shop in Portsmouth. There was a fair number of customers and the shopkeeper delighted in taking the mickey by refusing to understand a single word I said until I was forced to twist my tongue round the Queen's English as it is understood in Her Majesty's main realm. The strange thing is that, far from feeling bitter about the man's conduct, I felt guilty about not being able to speak in the accepted style. For me the English set the norms of speech and behaviour and anything different was obviously second rate. Quickly I learned to speak English. All around me I found Scots sailors who had made the same adjustment so the sense of having conformed to the proper way of speaking was unconsciously underlined.

My main training, which took about a year, was carried out at HMS Mercury, the naval signal school located on a beautiful estate up in the hills of Hampshire. The captain was Gordon-Lennox, who was later Serjeant-at-Arms in the House of Commons during my time there. The end of my course coincided with the Suez fiasco and I had a revealing glimpse of the mind of the minor Raj in the fading days of empire when, on the eve of hostilities, I escorted the duty officer on his inspection of the mess-decks. I picked him up at the wardroom where a celebration party was in full swing. My officer was drunk, loquacious and jingoistic.

When we had to wander round the estate going from mess-deck to mess-deck, he made mini-speeches to me. According to him the whole reason for the war was that the Gypos could not be trusted to run ships through the canal. They were hopeless without the guiding hand of the British. I thought privately that the Egyptians were just as likely to be good canal pilots as any other nationality but prudently I kept those views to myself.

When we hit the mess-decks it was Gilbertian. Normally on Navy "rounds", as the inspection is called, the officer does a quick trip round the mess to make sure it is clean and tidy, and then out again. Not on that night. Each mess got a major speech, which assured them that their moment of glory had arrived. We would sock it to the Gypos, put the upstart Nasser in his place and reassert England's natural role of leadership. I was glad to see the back of him and, a couple of days later, of HMS Mercury. On leaving training I was drafted to my first ship, a frigate, HMS Salisbury, at Devonport dockyard. We spent the Suez war doing trials before the final handover and, to my everlasting relief, we were not involved in the naval task force. The whole port was of course given over to the war effort and most ships were involved. My shipmates were all sorry about our non-combatant role and the atmosphere onboard was jingoistic. Our radio room, the bridge wireless office, was the source of all information, so people came to peer at the news coming over our teletypewriter. Nasser was denounced several times an hour. One day, when the dung was being heaped upon him for nationalising the Suez Canal, I remarked quite reasonably that there was nothing wrong with the Egyptians nationalising a waterway which ran through their own country. There was an explosion of anger during which the nicest thing said about me was that I was a "Gypo-loving bastard". That night, and on several other nights, I was threatened with a good going over.

12

Again do not get me wrong. I was far from being a fully fledged leftie of the lower deck. Both in training and during my early days at sea, I had no time for politics. The Navy was my life and while I had supported Nasser, I never realised that I was not an oddball and that in the world outside the Navy the Labour Party was in full opposition to Eden. The tussle between Macmillan and Butler after Eden's fall made no impression on me whatever. I did maintain my staunchly pro-trade union views in the face of anti-union bigotry which was rife in all ranks of the Navy. But by and large I was shut off from the world outside the service.

Sea duty proved a nightmare because of seasickness but I was essentially happy onboard. However, that came to an end in July 1957 when I was transferred to Hong Kong, where I was seconded to an Army unit in Kowloon. It was a special Royal Artillery unit set up to direct and co-ordinate naval gunfire in support of ground troops. I spent two-and-a-half years in Hong Kong and it transformed my whole outlook. The unit was mainly national servicemen, with four or five English public school products in their ranks, all of whom had wide-ranging cultural, political and sporting interests. There was also a number of regular soldiers who, like me, were misfits in a service world where beer, women, more beer and more women were the main topics of conversation. Birds of a feather came together. The English public school people were interesting and no doubt the slice of life we others presented to them was fascinating. Ultimately we found common interests and formed friendships. Most important, our mixed group was open to the influences which washed around the shores of Hong Kong and China at that time.

Hong Kong was then in the front line of the great ideological struggle conducted by the United States and Britain against Communist China. People poured into Hong Kong in a refugee flood, where they became the main raw material for the colony's new industrial base. They did not find much of a haven because exploitation, poverty and social stress were evident on every street and shanty town. On mainland China Mao Tse Tung was starting the Great Leap Forward. For anyone with a mind to look outside the barrack gates, it was a world full of interest and challenge. In an army unit little over thirty strong, half a dozen people with roughly the same interests can have a great sway; soon the barrackrooms were minor debating chambers.

It was in this setting, at the age of twenty, that I was first introduced to quality newspapers such as *The Observer* and *The Sunday Times*, which arrived in the colony around the Wednesday following publication in the UK. I had never heard of *The Scotsman* or the *Glasgow Herald*. The YWCA had a marvellous library (open to men) and the bookshops were full. A friend, Tony O'Donnell, got me to read Bertrand Russell and George Bernard Shaw: suddenly I began to look at the world, its problems, its peoples and their causes in a very new light. I devoured everything Russell produced for the general reader and read a bit of his philosophical works too, although it was hard going. I read all of Shaw's plays and prefaces. One of my English public school friends, a right-wing Tory, spent hours telling me about Bretton Woods, all of which was a revelation and a stimulus to learn more. It was wonderful discovering the world: in an untrained and unstructured way I began to explore it and myself. I read Marx and Engels, books about foreign and domestic policy, biographies and political history. The Royal Navy had long established educational courses which I had been aware of but previously ignored. Now I went in feet first, chasing GCE O-levels as did several other sailors in our unit.

Our small unit lived in a barracks run by a big regiment. They thought we were all a rum lot, including our officers. I suppose we were — even our officers were interested in politics. The CO had been captured by the Chinese in Korea and given a dose of political indoctrination. It only made him a more firmly entrenched anti-communist. However, he was a civilised and cultured man who would discuss his views with balance and respect for the opinions of others. His history and views emerged during the "current affairs" sessions he organised for the unit once a week. The second in command was only in the

14

army for the pay and privileges attached to being an officer. He was a bit on the lazy side and easy going, fancying himself as a bit of a Labour man, taking Ernie Bevin as his hero. The young officers were on national service: one was a wine merchant and another, his successor, aimed to become a Church of England minister. Neither felt strongly about their rank, both being on national service — so we were free and easy in discussions. It all made for a good, although in the military sense unusual, atmosphere. Of supreme importance was the self-confidence I was developing, based upon the realisation that I was able to assimilate facts and ideas and form them into a coherent personal and political philosophy which could be defended in debate against obviously well-educated, articulate people.

Politically, I was tempted towards communism and even wrote a letter to the old *Daily Worker* which they never published. China was on our doorstep and there was no question that Mao Tse Tung had lifted his people out of backward squalor and exploitation. I was an uncritical supporter of the Great Leap Forward and saw this immensely strong man and his party's central role as essential to real economic and social advancement for the Chinese people whom I had come to admire from observing them on the streets of Hong Kong. Communist centralism, with its drumbeat of absolute certainty and claim to infallibility in the interpretation of history and forecast of the future, had an astonishing attraction for me.

Bertrand Russell stopped me from becoming a communist. His strictures on a creed which could mangle the human intellect and marked down human casualties as "historical costs" in the accounts of revolution and post-revolutionary change, took me back into the democratic fold. I admired Mao Tse Tung but came to hate Stalin. However, the attraction of strong centralist action as a means of tackling great problems remained undiminished. I was a firm democratic centralist.

In all those thirty months in the colony, I can recall only one debate about Scotland as distinct from Britain. Two of us from

Scotland got hotly involved with an English soldier who was holding forth on how the English subsidised the Celts. Somewhere deep inside the blood boiled and we argued with more passion than fact that Scotland was easily a viable entity. Whether we really believed what we said, or simply felt it necessary to uphold some Scottish dignity, I cannot now say. The incident stayed in my memory, but it was small beer compared with the big issues which engaged us daily — the growing tension between the West and China, the rise of the non- aligned movement, the question of Cypriot independence, the Hola death camp in Kenya and the great ideological clash between socialism and capitalism.

At Christmas 1959 I returned from Hong Kong and a couple of months later left the Navy, having bought my discharge. I had served five out of a nine-year contract but I was by then married with a young son: my political development was not compatible with life in a Navy dominated by the class system. I never regretted joining the Navy and I have retained an affection for the service, believing I owe it a great deal in the way I was trained and for the experience I gained.

Anyway, I came back from Hong Kong a different person, well read in politics and imbued with a desire to help in the British and international working-class struggle. Some might say a good example of a little knowledge being dangerous. Others, more charitably, would recognise a late developer developing fast. There were still problems of articulation of thought and my lack of attendance at Ayr Academy left me with a woefully inadequate vocabulary. I was still frequently stuck for the right words. But by then I knew how to search a dictionary and found great pleasure in adding to my store of words.

Back in Scotland and out of the Navy, within a few months I was a member of the Kilmarnock Fire Brigade and a member of the Fire Brigades Union. The FBU was a highly political outfit, led by John Horner, a man with magnificent oratorial skills allied to a first-class mind. He was a Londoner, had been a senior member of the British Communist Party, but was by 1960 a member of the Labour Party. We had good leadership at local levels too so as a new member I was given a warm and friendly reception. Within a few weeks I was branch chairman and shortly after that became area chairman and delegate to the Scottish District Committee.

Two men dominated the Scottish district. Alex Napier from Musselburgh was secretary and Enoch Humphries from Cambuslang was the chairman. Enoch was later to become president of the union and also of the Scottish TUC. Alex was a thoughtful man, with great patience, who saw the trade union not only as an instrument for the present but as a continuing institution representing all that was best, not just for firemen, but the whole of the working class. He was unfailing in his encouragement of young lads like me. Enoch Humphries was very different: he bustled and his quick mind was combined with an aggressive style. As a negotiating team they were perfect and I was happy to sit at their feet and learn. Negotiating national standards of wages for the Fire Service was at that time quite difficult. The employers were a mix of local authority joint boards covering urban, rural and city areas (including London), coming together in a single national body. In almost every brigade, except London, there were long waiting lists for jobs. By the laws of supply and demand, to which even socialist negotiators had to pay notice, the union was on weak ground in wringing more cash out of the National Joint Council employers' side. The London brigade was desperately short of men and, with London's economy going through a boom, only increased wages could attract recruits to its ranks. London had, in the employers' eyes, a good case whereas the rest of us had no case.

The delicate problem for the union leadership was how to use the London situation as a lever for raising wages in the rest of the country. There had, of course, always been a London weighting allowance on top of basic salaries but it was not a huge amount. The union's case to the employers rested upon the need to increase substantially London wage levels, while not creating too big a gap between that brigade and the rest, thereby doing moral justice to men who manned the provinces. The union argued that such a settlement would avoid serious loss of morale that would become inevitable if London became a super-brigade, while the hicks elsewhere got thrown buttons. The employers knew the score and did their best to split the union. They offered London almost everything they needed, while giving other brigades very little on the grounds that if we did not like it then there were plenty of men on the waiting lists who would take our jobs on the conditions we rejected.

In that situation, the members of the London branches of the FBU were all-important. If they wanted to cut and run, nothing could have stopped them. They did not. Every London fireman knew his importance to others and, despite the obvious temptations, the London district stood firmly by the national union on a point of principle. In the end it was a messy business with a compromise forced upon us by government policy. We retained a national wage structure but London got a bigger than usual payment as a weighting. The result left tensions within the union in which Glasgow, and not London, represented the main threat to unity. Those of us in brigades such as the South-West of Scotland, Aberdeen and Renfrewshire felt greater kinship and harmony with our London colleagues than with our Glasgow friends near at hand. London had been used as a willing lever accepting less than they knew was available from an autonomous deal with the employers. Glasgow, on the other hand, was demanding a kind of supplement to the national agreement for themselves alone. They did this on the spurious grounds that their fires were more dangerous and difficult than those fought by others in the towns and rural areas. To the unaware public this might have seemed the case because Glasgow fires could be more spectacular than in other areas — to professional firemen in Kilmarnock, Aberdeen or Dumfries this was known to be a nonsense.

In those years of developing strife the union needed a strong central body to hold it together against the forces at work in a service which, in its day-to-day life, was highly decentralised and therefore likely to fall apart. The ideas I had picked up on the borders of China and from the works of Marxist scholars about the benefits of strong central authority were again underlined by my union experience.

In 1962 I suffered an accident which made my right knee useless so I was compulsorily retired from the fire brigade. My work in the FBU had taken me into the Labour Party and I had become secretary of the constituency Labour Party and part-time election agent: it seemed quite logical to everyone that if I had to leave the fire brigade then I should work full time for the party. Shortly after taking up the post, I joined Ayr Town Council and became the close confidant of the group leader, Charlie O'Halloran, who later became convener of Strathclyde Regional Council and left politics as Sir Charles. In those days Charlie was a rival of Alex Eadie for the Labour parliamentary nomination for the Ayr constituency. He would often ridicule Alex Eadie's MBE: his friends, including myself, felt he was one man who would spurn the honours of a capitalist society. How naïve!

In those days, the early 1960s, the idea of democratic centralism held sway in the Labour Party. The old debates about self-government were past long before I joined and centralist ideas were well entrenched. Hugh Gaitskell was leader but in Ayrshire we were a left-wing area, with a strong ILP influence taking us into opposition to the leadership on public ownership and nuclear disarmament. The older generation of socialists, who had fought back from the disaster of 1931, were still in charge in most of the county's small burghs, in Kilmarnock and in the landward districts. The County Council was run by Danny Sim, the County Convener, an incorruptible ex-miner of ability, who commanded universal respect, but was certainly not liked by everyone.

The Macmillan government was running into trouble. There was a rising mood of confidence in the movement, despite the battles over nuclear disarmament and there was a wide agreement on Labour's economic programme set out in a policy document, *Signposts for the Sixties*, which was founded on centralist concepts. But so firm was the centralist belief in the party that I doubt if all but a few noticed that characteristic. Never once, in the many official discussions I took part in, did the question of devolution ever come up. We were all concerned with ideological issues such as the need to direct capital and whether instruments of national planning would be strong enough to deal with the growing power of big business. There was a special Scottish edition of *Signposts*, and its remarkably nationalist tone was accepted without anyone noticing the contradictions between its sentiments and its adherence to British centralist planning. Indeed at that time the Scottish element of the party had a good conceit of itself. While Macmillan was sweeping the rest of the UK in 1959, Scotland had registered a substantial swing to Labour. The Scottish front bench opposition never lost an opportunity to rub that fact into the Tories. Many speeches made in the country by Labour MPs ran along the lines that the Scottish Tories were an anglicised lot whose affinity with all things English forfeited any right to Scottish electoral support. As the SNP was not even a speck on the horizon, one can only conclude that this unconscious nationalism was real, although the direction in which it pointed, to some form of self-government, was exactly the opposite to what the party was promising. We all lived happily with this, blissful in our ignorance.

There was, I remember, one discordant voice. A man who bored the pants off everyone at the 1962 Scottish Labour Conference. He went from one group to another around the bars at the civic reception, going on and on about the need for a Scottish Parliament. He had a thoroughly unpleasant evening as people finally told him to push off. He was Andrew Hargreave, a top financial correspondent and a member of the party. Someone I later came to realise as a political analyst of the first rank. On that occasion, however, he was just a nuisance.

With the death of Hugh Gaitskell, we got a new leader in Harold Wilson. With his speeches about forging a new Britain in the white heat of the technological revolution, he captured the imagination of the party and, we thought, of the country. The mechanics of change spilled out of Wilson, with "powerful" and "purposive" being common adjectives describing the economic system by which a new Labour government would transform the country. Again, there was the centralist theme. Power was concentrated in a capitalist society, and a strong central socialist government was needed to bend and break that power. That was our view.

When the 1964 election was called I was election agent in Ayr for Alex Eadie, fighting George Younger. Although I had voted for Charlie O'Halloran at the Ayr selection conference, I was happy to work with Alex who was the victor. We established a close and firm friendship that lasted for many years.

Becoming an election agent on a full-time basis was important in shaping my attitudes. Being a full-time bureaucrat meant putting the organisation and its success before everything else. In practice one learned to suppress individual opinions and promote the corporate viewpoint, especially as set out by the leadership. I was on my way to becoming a proficient party hack. As a loyal party hack I defended the July measures of 1966 when a Labour government with over 100 of a majority opted for deflation and, for the first time ever, legitimised the use of unemployment as an economic tool of management. At the general meeting of the Ayr Constituency Labour Party I routed the NUM delegate by a debating point, ridiculing his call for the nationalisation of the Bank of England by explaining that his objective had been accomplished by Attlee! I used his error as an example of how critics were speaking from ignorance while *our* government was facing realities. While the meeting turned out to be a "success" in that the government's critics were heavily defeated in the vote, I had sensed an air of unease among delegates. Afterwards, reviewing my own thoughts, I felt unclean. I made a private promise never again to sin my soul. I knew that in politics compromise was necessary, and that there would be times when the unpalatable would have to be swallowed, but I would not stand on my head ever again.

There was no significance in that decision outside of my own being. Ayr had no Labour MPs, none of us were on any national party body and our opinions counted for little anywhere except within our own small area. But it was important for my personal development and for my view of Harold Wilson. My previous uncritical admiration for him evaporated and I intensely disliked what his twisting and turning had made me do.

Wilson's years in the leadership proved to be the poison which destroyed the credit, integrity and ultimately the decency and vitality of the Labour Party. By 1967 the Wilson rot was well set in and we faced a bye-election at Pollok in Glasgow. I was drafted in as one of the team of full-time organisers and for the first time came across a highly visible nationalist campaign. The Tory won and Labour came second — but the big talking point was the good result for the SNP.

Later that year the Hamilton bye-election saw Winnie Ewing turn a safe Labour seat into an SNP marginal, with the help of significant tactical voting by Tories and the transfer of a big slice of the Labour vote. It was like an earthquake inside the Labour Party and knees wobbled everywhere. The aftermath was fantastic with the SNP, soaring in membership and credibility, coming from nowhere to completely dominate the Scottish scene. Having run the Scottish Tories off the park in the years leading up to 1966, Labour was complacent and nowhere more so than in so-called safe seats. There was also a feeling of disillusionment with the performance of the Labour government. There was a crisis of confidence in the party, now faced with a nationalist opposition which was fresh, different, exciting and full of conviction.

By this time, I was secretary of the Ayrshire Labour Federation, which embraced every Labour Party and trade union in the county. John Pollock, now general secretary of the Education Institute of Scotland, was chairman. My first reaction to the Hamilton result was clearly stated in an occasional letter I put out for the Federation. The thinking and the tone will surprise some people. It was published on 9 November 1969 and here are some extracts:

The first lesson from Hamilton is this: if a party does not actively pursue the electorate's support by carrying its policy to them it will lose votes, and deserve to lose votes. If one can digress for a moment, this mistake will not be found anywhere in Ayrshire. Just two weeks before Hamilton, the Irvine Labour Party with a fighting campaign sunk the SNP to the bottom of the poll where he collected only 77 votes.

They [SNP] will be able to rely less and less on slogans and emotion, and forced to come through more and more with clear-cut statements on the ways and means by which they will achieve independence. The signs are that they will not be able to carry out this complex and difficult exercise. . . .

It is significant that faced with the responsibility of being an MP (and not merely a candidate), Mrs Ewing could only remark on Friday morning that the question of getting more jobs for Scotland was a very difficult problem.

Now to the question of "temporary revolt". If the Nationalists are as wrong as I make out, why did they poll such a high vote and why is there a growing feeling in Scotland that we need a bigger say in our own affairs?

The Nationalists were bound to get a very very high vote, whatever Labour said or did at Hamilton, because at the moment they are the only means open to people to register what is a genuine and legitimate feeling in Scotland (as in Wales) that we should handle much more of our domestic life, and would do so for the better of our nation.

The real lesson of Hamilton is that Labour must recognise this as a fact. There is much in Scottish life that could be, and should be dealt with here. We have our own laws, local government, educational system and other matters distinctly Scottish. And it is nonsense that changes in these should wait their turn in the queue for legislative time at Westminster.

This was recognised in many Labour circles well before Hamilton. The result there will now act as a spur towards a greater degree of devolution. The Labour Party will not ignore the obvious feelings of our people and new measures are bound to be forthcoming. They will, however, in the interests of

> of economic sanity not go to the lengths of "independence" advocated by the Nationalists.

This was in Labour terms, an impeccable devolutionist's statement and a remarkable attitude from someone steeped in the centralist tradition. How then did its author shortly thereafter emerge as the "Hammer of the Nats", and come down hard against any truck with a Scottish Parliament? Step forward Mrs Winnie Ewing.

What happened was that Winnie went on a grand tour of Scotland which, as well as inflating SNP membership, also inflated her self-regard. Her speeches indicated a growing conviction that not a single person before her, with the brief exception of Robert McIntyre, had ever been really concerned for the Scottish people. The circus finally came to Ayr when she spoke at the racecourse, in a building, not on the track. The hall was packed. I was there with young Alex Neil, then in his final year of study at Ayr Academy, and with Eddie Murray, the Labour County Councillor for Annbank. A good part of Winnie's speech was a particularly venomous and offensive onslaught on the Labour Party. We bristled, as she listed our "crimes" against the Scottish people and as she sneered at our efforts over generations. It was an ignorant attack against men and women we knew to have fought a great struggle against Toryism and who had broken the landed gentry's grip upon the working people of Ayrshire. No man I have ever known cared more deeply about the people than did Danny Sim. The County Labour Group was full of folk like Willie Paterson of Logan, Helen Nisbet of Catrine, old blind Willie Love from the Irvine Valley, Jimmie Reid who had been one of the courageous pacifists to stand against the military madness of 1914-18 and Annie Mackie who worried more about all the families of Kilmarnock than she did about herself. These, and others, had all given selflessly in public service. It was service with no return except the satisfaction of providing decent houses in place of slums, jobs in place of despair, educational opportunities for all and trade union rights to protect the dignity of labour. As Mrs

Ewing boasted of her own virtues and poured scorn upon the kind of people I knew and respected, my balanced approach penned in the Federation newsletter went out of the window. We left the meeting seething, determined to fix her and her like. There would be no accommodation, no compromise, no quarter asked or given. The small opening in my centralist mind closed like a trapdoor.

Looking back some years later I saw that our reaction to Mrs Ewing, particularly my own, was not rational. Whatever the woman said should not have altered my view of the circumstances that gave rise to Hamilton and the upsurge in support for the SNP. I should have pursued a line of objective reasoning. However, even now admitting my error, I can still understand how and why that error was made. It is worth digressing for a short spell on this because the SNP has still not learned that a certain style of attack on the Labour movement can be counterproductive.

The Labour Party is the most important institution in the history of the working people and that part of the intelligentsia which gives itself to progressive causes. Labour was not born in a vacuum but emerged from a movement of struggle for justice which had its roots buried in the formative years of the industrial revolution. The heartbreak, the sense of solidarity, and the stepping-stone victories of that struggle are in its genes. Even although it is a twentieth-century creation, it is in direct descent from the poor, their leaders and their sacrifices of previous times. There is too the history of success to which the Labour Party can lay claim. At parliamentary and local government level, Labour has been central to the advancement made in housing, education, the welfare services and the creation of an atmosphere in which concern for people can flourish. While the parliamentary scene atttracts the glamour, the main practical achievements have been at local level.

Generalised attacks upon the Labour Party when the target should be the Parliamentary Labour Party (by far the least popular element and the most open to indictment) can too easily be taken as denigration of the whole Labour movement and its history. People will reject attempts to blacken a party if their contact with the organisation is a local person, or shop steward, all too obviously working hard for the general good of the community. Listeners to a tirade simply cannot associate the devilish targets with those they know to be good people and so you get, at best, switch-off. At worst, you get a strong hostile reaction, more particularly from activists who see and feel things in much sharper tone than does the general public.

I reacted badly, as did many others, to Winnie's jibes and sneers. It has been fashionable for Winnie Ewing to complain that she was badly treated at a personal level in Parliament from 1967 to 1970. There is much justice in her claim and she has certainly convinced the majority of SNP members that she was unfairly abused. But she forgets that her strident brand of crowing and the insults she dealt out all over Scotland were the origin of that treatment.

In Ayrshire we decided to fight back. Simultaneously, I was in touch with a number of people who felt we must do something to steady the party's nerves. We decided on a pamphlet and a group met in Hamish McKinven's house in the Edinburgh area. This was in late 1967. Hamish was the party's part-time press officer. I cannot now recall all who took part in the meeting but John Mackintosh was there, as was Alex Eadie and Jack Kane, the leader of the Edinburgh Labour group. By then Alex Eadie was MP for Midlothian. John Mackintosh wanted Willie Ross out of office because in John's view he was a public relations disaster as Secretary of State. There was no way anyone from Ayrshire, despite our disagreements with him, would campaign for the removal of Ross. Why? Because we saw the man's virtues as well as his faults. He had integrity; he, not the civil servants, ran the Scottish Office; he was known to fight like a tiger inside the Cabinet for any advantage he sought for Scotland ("Tartan Willie" was Barbara Castle's name for him). The removal of Ross would diminish the influence of the Ayrshire Labour Federation which had a direct line through to the Secretary of State — something no other group had. At the end of a bad meeting, we nevertheless decided to write a pamphlet attacking the nationalists which would reject a claim for self-government. John Mackintosh could not go along with that. However, Jack Kane and Alex Eadie agreed to consider a draft once it was available. I was given the task of writing it.

That was the background to *Don't Butcher Scotland's Future*, which became a best-selling pamphlet dealing blow after blow at the SNP's main plank of a Scottish Parliament. Having gone back quickly into my centralist position, following the Winnie Ewing public meeting, I had no problem writing the pamphlet. Once written, however, only Alex Eadie would sign, so we put it out in our two names. To my genuine astonishment the pamphlet caught fire and was in great demand. So were Alex and myself as speakers at various public and private meetings organised by hitherto demoralised Labour parties in all parts of Scotland. Shortly afterwards, I wrote a much better polemic, *Exposed: the Truth about the SNP*, which sold like hot cakes. The nationalists reacted and I received the usual hate mail and an allocation of excreta through the post. Challenges were thrown around to debate and all were accepted by me.

The most difficult debate was with Oliver Brown, in the autumn of 1968, in the McLellan Galleries in Glasgow. Oliver had challenged Alex Eadie but he declined. Oliver wrote to me, the second and lesser string. My friends advised against it, saying I was not yet capable of taking on one of the most experienced and able political minds in the country, a master of devastating quip. After Hamilton it was Oliver who remarked: "A shiver ran along the Scottish Labour benches looking for a spine to run up." But you cannot write a pamphlet and refuse to debate — running away from the nationalists would intensify and not solve Labour's main problems of loss of confidence and conviction. Anyway, I had debated with other SNP people and not found them formidable. So I accepted.

The hall was crowded. As I came in I heard Annie Welsh, the

organiser of the Cumnock SNP, say she had brought a bus-load because they wanted to see this over-confident Labour so-and-so thumped. In the debate, I did not find Oliver Brown over-whelming and formed an instant liking for the man. The audience, who were mainly nationalists with a sprinkling of socialists, had come to see a slaughter. They were in an ugly mood when the blood did not spill and at the end Oliver informed me, seriously, that his main difficulty was to get me out of the hall unscathed. He managed it, just.

The whole episode of the pamphlet, the debates and the letter campaigns in national newspapers had made me a minor public figure and my reputation caught the attention of some people on the General Council of the Scottish Trades Union Congress. A vacancy had arisen when Jim Craigen, now MP for Maryhill, left the post of Head of Organisation and Social Services Department. My old FBU friend, Enoch Humphries, was a member of the General Council and persuaded me to apply. I was given the job in 1968.

My time at the STUC proved to be another significant influence on my development. At that time the STUC was very much at the centre of Scottish affairs and the whole trade union movement was about to become embroiled with Barbara Castle over *In Place of Strife*. The STUC's reputation was high. George Middleton, who retired from the General Secretaryship in the early 1960s, was a remarkable personality who stamped himself and the STUC on the public mind. His successor, Jimmy Jack, was different. He was introspective and always seemed to feel unsafe. This was a hangover from his work under Middleton, when George cast such a big shadow that no one else could be seen. Jimmy's private dislike of Middleton was so great that he would never occupy the General Secretary's office, which was across the landing from the boardroom. Instead, he remained in one of the two small offices in the top floor. This left first Jim Craigen and then me with the best accommodation.

Jimmy Jack underrated himself. He had a good intellect and a sound grasp of economics, much more so than Middleton. He knew the importance of founding a case on facts which would still stand when the rhetoric was only a faint echo and thus brought substance and solidity to the work and image of the STUC. Jimmy expected a quality and reasoned judgement from his staff and I always found him willing to spend time in discussing and analysing a subject. His ear was well tuned to what the workers thought and felt and it was he who started pulling the STUC away from a Unionist to a devolutionary stance. His talks with me on the subject of self-government, when I was safely away from the pressures of keeping up morale in my part of the Labour Party and could therefore think instead of merely reacting, had an effect. He helped soften my approach, made me research the subject and held out the STUC as a classic example of where an autonomous Scottish institution could and did work to the benefit of Scotland, without doing down any other section of the British working class.

In 1968, the General Council decided to set out its views on devolution to the Congress which was scheduled to convene at Rothesay in April 1969. The General Council was also required to set out its definitive view on the Donovon Royal Commission's *Report on Trade Unions and Employers' Associations* and on *In Place of Strife*. Both reports fell into my remit for production in draft form. Understandably, given my known public attitudes, Jimmy Jack took the drafting of the devolution statement into his own office, leaving me with what proved to be the much more controversial issue of the industrial relations statement.

At the Congress, the STUC document was passed overwhelmingly, committing the trade union movement to support for some form of Assembly. It was a big step forward for an important part of the Labour movement and I was not unhappy with the case put forward or the outcome. I greatly enjoyed life in the back rooms of the STUC and I found working in the trade union movement more satisfying than the political field. It was an interesting place to be as the nation swung nationalist. It was, too, a particularly important period in which events north of the border, in the political field with the rise of the SNP, determined a new relationship between the STUC and the TUC.

The STUC always had to struggle for survival against the TUC. There were two main reasons for this. First, the STUC had been created in reaction to a decision by the TUC to remove trades councils from direct representation to the policy-making congress. The trades council movement, which represented the rank and file, was strong in Scotland at that time. There was a firm intention among the rank and file not to be excluded from direct national participation in matters affecting trade unionists and from that attitude the Scottish TUC was formed, with individual unions and all trades councils holding the right of direct representation at the Scottish congress. By forming the STUC the Scots did not break away from the TUC. They continued, through their unions, to play a role in that body but had the dual benefit of their autonomous congress. This declaration of difference was not welcomed at TUC headquarters in London and for many years the STUC was a source of irritation. There was always a hope in the TUC mind that the irritant would not survive. Second, the Scottish section of the movement had always been to the left of the TUC. That meant the STUC, especially with rank-and-file representation through the trades councils, sang a different tune on most policies to that of the TUC. This was of importance during the decades when the TUC was right-wing dominated. At the TUC they could crush the left, only to see it reappear at the autonomous congress in Scotland. Given this background of hidden tension, hidden because few commentators ever bothered to probe below the surface, Scots trade union leaders believed their best chance of survival and growth lay in a policy of quietly but tenaciously hanging on.

When the Scottish dimension in British life burst forth in 1967 with the Hamilton bye-election result, one of its by-products was to buttress the position of the Scottish TUC. It was Enoch Humphries, president of the STUC in 1968-69, who said to me outside the offices after a meeting on Jimmy Jack's devolution document, "One thing they [the SNP] have done is secure our position against the TUC." I remember the words as if spoken a few minutes ago. With the STUC reaching a new level of importance, it was impossible not to recognise that for all the difficulties inherent in the relationship with the TUC inside a unitary trade union movement, a separate Scottish institution could advance the cause of the Scottish working people without in any way endangering and weakening the cause of British labour. Working at the centre of trade union activity in Scotland, I could not fail but be influenced by my experience of that reality.

My trade union work was cut short, however, when the Labour MP for South Ayrshire, Emrys Hughes, died in late 1969. Everyone's first choice was John Pollock, but he declined. Charlie O'Halloran wanted the seat but had no personal support in the constituency. Councillor Willie Goudie of New Cumnock won the NUM nomination. I was put in to stop Goudie and did so by one vote at the selection conference.

*Chapter 2*

# LABOUR MP

THE SOUTH AYRSHIRE bye-election was held in February/
March of 1970. My main opponent was a formidable man, Sam
Purdie of the SNP, in many ways my political twin. Sam had
been a rising star in Labour South Ayrshire. He worked in
the pits and had been Emrys Hughes's election agent while
I was election agent in Ayr. He was very much a product
of the trade union movement: he had applied to enter Ruskin
College at Oxford and was accepted, whereas I had applied
and been rejected. Sam, like me, was a socialist. His decision
to leave the Labour Party and become SNP candidate was an
obvious agony for him, while it was an outrage to many Labour
colleagues of his.

Early in the campaign I took a great risk in accepting a
challenge to debate with Sam. The Cumnock Town Hall had
standing room only, with a good part of the audience there to
listen before deciding on how to vote. Sam lost the debate
because, at a critical point, he refused three times to answer a
point blank question: are you still a socialist? Had he answered
"yes" and gone on to claim that only through Home Rule could
we gain a socialist Scotland, I was in trouble. But the SNP
strategy was to win votes from every corner — from the Tory
farmers around Girvan, the cautious middle-of-the-road folk in
Maybole and from the socialists in the Doon Valley and the
Cumnock district. To declare himself a socialist, and thus signal
what kind of Scotland he really sought, meant Sam could not
cast his net wide enough — or so he thought. What he and the

SNP did not realise was that the majority, the Labour vote, were concerned with the economic and social changes that would flow from constitutional change and not simply constitutional change for its own sake.

In the Doon Valley and Cumnock, a candidate had no chance if he refused to declare for socialism. That was the moment Sam was beaten and from then until polling day Labour had a happy, joyful and successful campaign. I hammered the idea of a separate Scotland, but did concede that it would be prudent to wait until the Royal Commission on the Constitution had considered the issue of devolution before finally accepting or rejecting something less than independence. I won with a majority of 10,886 votes, with the Tories second.

Going to Westminster in March 1970, as a new MP, held no excitement for me. Nor was I awed by the place. Having been a full-time Labour agent, I had seen MPs at their best, and worst, and I viewed Parliament less as an institution than a workplace in which we should beat out the policies to elevate the working people. My first few weeks were filled in getting used to the place, mastering the English public school debating style and watching the build-up of hysteria when a tremendous surge of support in the opinion polls pushed Harold Wilson into cutting and running for a June election.

That election was an anti-climax in South Ayrshire as the bye-election was still fresh in people's minds. The polls said there would be another Labour government so the three-week campaign rolled gently along. A few hours after the polls closed, the real ones as distinct from the opinion polls, Heath was in and Wilson was out, although Labour was triumphant in Scotland. South Ayrshire counted on the Friday morning so by the time we all gathered at the county buildings it was more of a wake than a celebration of my increased majority tumbling out of the ballot boxes. Even more harrowing was the short speech made by Sam Purdie who fought me for a second time and lost his deposit. Labour had polled 23,910 votes whereas Sam Purdie had only 3,103.

My own victory speech was designed to lift the spirits of Labour supporters in the big crowd gathered to hear the result. I promised that, along with Ayrshire's other Labour MPs, Ross and Lambie, we would fight the Tories every inch of the way and that one setback was no rout. I was optimistic about the future. At the tail came Sam, who said: "I don't know what Mr Sillars is so happy about. His party has just swept the board in Scotland again but we now have a Tory government that we didn't vote for." My private reaction was "Thank God he didn't say things like that during the bye-election because I frankly don't know the answer to it". Sam's speech haunted me and its logic was confirmed in the week following the election when I gave a miner a lift on his way to Killoch colliery. The miner said: "Why should we put up with an English Tory government Jim when we're a Labour country up here?" I offered a few placatory remarks about us not being blown off course with one defeat, but I was privately seriously disturbed.

I followed the Purdie line when Parliament took up its work, as you will see from this exchange between me and Heath, who was Prime Minister:

> *Mr Sillars:* When the Prime Minister goes to Scotland tomorrow, will he look up the election results for 1970 and understand that, because he issued a separate manifesto for Scotland and Scotland voted overwhelmingly for Labour, it is claptrap for him and his Ministers to say that they have a mandate for cutting Scottish public expenditure and destroying the Labour government's investment grants scheme?
> *The Prime Minister:* Scotland is part of the United Kingdom and intends to remain so. Policies are pursued by the United Kingdom Government. We shall carry out the policy that we pledged to Scotland.

There were hearty Labour cheers and the greatest encouragement came from the man sitting next to me. "You tell him, Jim. That's right," said Eric Heffer. I remember it well.

My next course was to try and get the executive of the Scottish Labour group of MPs to examine the implications of our big majority and the argument that the Tories had no mandate in Scotland. Members of the executive were happy to dodge the issue and that effort came to nothing. Meanwhile the Tories were trying to push through their Industrial Relations Bill and I was deeply involved in the PLP steering group opposing it line by line inside the House of Commons and lending political support at meetings and demonstrations organised by the TUC and STUC. To stop the Tory assault on the British trade union movement was the number one priority, although economic and political issues affecting Scotland were far from neglected.

Those were the years of the UCS work-in and the years of the STUC all-Scotland assemblies to protest against rising unemployment. This latter development was very important and caused me to think ever more deeply about the solutions to the problems facing working people in my own country. The flavour of the first and most important STUC assembly can be gleaned from this extract of Chris Baur's report in *The Scotsman*, 15 February 1972:

> Scotland took a historic and irrevocable step towards self-government yesterday. It was Mr James Jack, General Secretary of the Scottish TUC, who summed up the peculiar meaning of yesterday's remarkable Scottish Assembly on un-employment in Edinburgh.
>
> In a statement punctuated by the cheering and applause of many of the 1,500 people who went to the Usher Hall, he said: "The road we are taking may take us finally to a Scottish Parliament."
>
> He continued: "And I say to those who respond to the suggestion of a Scottish Parliament, I am all for it because — wait for it" as he was again interrupted by clapping, "because there is not the slightest doubt in my mind that a Scottish Parliament would be a workers' Parliament."

Later in his report, Chris Baur noted that the CBI's Scottish Secretary, Hamish Grant, saw support for a Parliament as a statement of the obvious: "It was noticeable that speaker after speaker maintained the theme of the need for Scotland to be given greater responsibility for the management of her own affairs by the devolution of more responsibility to Scottish institutions." Thus spake the CBI. Chris Baur saw the most "notable" conversion as that of John Boyd, the engineering union leader and arch-opponent of Scottish Nationalist solutions. Boyd said: "I am slowly and painfully coming to the conclusion that the only answer to Scotland's economic problem is Scottish government." I was mentioned as having given aid and comfort to the idea and Mrs Winnie Ewing finished off the article for Chris Baur, saying: "This is a candle lit after a long dark night. It is quite possible that out of this power may come again to Scotland so that you will never get your priorities wrong again."

With the two strands, British and Scottish, intertwined in my thoughts I struggled to find a principled position after Sam Purdie had kicked away my confidence in June 1970. It was a struggle of conflicting concepts: one day addressing a group of trade unionists in the London area, drawing on the history of the British movement to illustrate the significance of the trade union opposition to Heath's Industrial Relations Bill and the next day being told bluntly by a West Midlands Labour MP that he would demolish regional policy whenever the chance came because he thought his area had given too much to Scotland anyway. Looking back and reading some old press clippings, I must have given the impression of the continued confidence that so infuriated Annie Welsh of the Cumnock SNP. But just below the surface I was confused. Moreover there was the question of the EEC, with British entry, in my view, pushing Scotland further away from the influential centres of decision-making.

In an effort to untangle my thoughts I wrote a lengthy memorandum, just a private and personal review. By then Harry Ewing had won a bye-election at Falkirk, Stirling and Grangemouth constituency and he, along with Alex Eadie and myself, made up a close threesome, sharing the same digs in London. They had a look at the memorandum and commented favourably. Later I handed it to Willie Ross to read as we

36

departed from London on the late sleeper one Thursday night. Around 6.00 a.m. the next morning, as we got off at Kilmarnock, he handed it back with the memorable comment: "It's very good, but what are you worrying about the SNP for, they are finished." As we walked down the hill to the bus station for the final lap of the journey to Ayr, I tried to explain that my concern was not about the SNP but the condition of the Scottish people. Ross is a most difficult man to engage in a dialogue unless he is telling you something. I got nowhere with him.

The following passage from that memorandum, dated February 1972, will show the influences at work:

> Now that growth has come, it may be that as well as being too little it is too late. Another obstacle to the achievement of regional policies has arisen in the nationwide unemployment we face.
>
> Whereas before the difficulty in regional policies lay in not having enough industry wanting to move from, say, the Midlands, we now face the situation that industry dare not be allowed to move from such areas.
>
> Previously prosperous areas are now suffering high unemployment. The longer we endure figures of around the one million mark, the more acute the problem will become in these hitherto full employment parts of England and the greater will be the industrial and political pressures on government to retain industry and encourage expansion and new industry to locate itself there.
>
> The outlook for Scotland within the UK, if the above analysis is correct, is, therefore, not good. The outlook could only be improved by a British Labour government pursuing economic policies of a type which were never contemplated by the last Labour government.
>
> There seem to be three courses open to Scotland. One is to remain an integral part of the UK. One is to achieve a measure of devolution. The third is to set up a separate state.
>
> Arguments for a measure of devolution are attractive, of course. They offer the best of both worlds, or appear to. But if devolution means no more than that we can achieve a marginal extension of our present limited powers to strengthen the Scottish part of the UK economy, then it would add little to our ability to overcome deep-seated problems.

If the desire is to exert a massive degree of Scottish control over Scottish economic life, then devolution is not the solution we can seek. Devolution would give us the form but not the substance of economic control. Centrally taken decisions at a UK level would still be the crucial decisions.

If devolution is set aside we are left with two extremes: continuing in unity with England as we are, or becoming separate.

This paper's analysis of Scotland's future as part of the UK shows it to be bleak. It may well be that the coming outline analysis of attempts to run Scotland as a separate entity will show a similarly bleak outlook or possibly a worse outlook.

I am quoting at length from this private memorandum, which was written without correction as my mind tumbled out its thoughts. Readers will notice that there is no mention of oil. Some English critics always claimed that I changed when the oil began to flow but, as this memorandum demonstrates, as did the many contributions at the STUC assembly, nationalist feeling preceded the oil bonanza. Indeed in paragraph 24 of my memorandum I describe the SNP stories about oil at that time as "fraudulent" and believed them to be so and so dismissed the oil issue.

The rest of the paper consisted of a detailed examination of the case for separation and the difficulties inherent in establishing a genuinely independent economy after over two centuries of integration. My conclusion was:

While Scotland would be independent in the academic sense, there would be definite limitations on the degree of freedom that she could exercise.

But I drew no final conclusions. This mattered less than the fact that I had sat down and written over 3,000 words in a personal and honest examination of a matter that had come to plague me daily. Whatever else I might be, I was definitely no longer a unionist.

While these constitutional issues were passed over and over in my mind, I was taking greater interest in economic affairs. Previously I had hesitated, thinking that this was chiefly the sphere for well-trained minds and great intellects such as Wilson, Heath, Jenkins, Crosland, Ian Macleod, Enoch Powell and the like. In those days, early in my parliamentary life, I spent a lot of time in the House of Commons debating chamber, listening as the great men addressed each other. I read a great deal also and received much needed guidance and assistance from John Robertson, Labour MP for Paisley. John had teamed up with Alex Eadie, Harry Ewing and myself.

John Robertson had been the victor of the Paisley bye-election of 1961 but had made little mark in Parliament. By the time I reached the House of Commons, John was sunk in political gloom, going through the motions of being an MP. He was openly despised by Willie Ross; his opinion was rarely sought and no one listened to his speeches. The snobbish clan who ran the Scottish group in the early and late 'sixties, Peggie Herbison, Willie Ross, Tom Fraser, and supporting players like George Lawson of Motherwell, successfully shouldered John out into the cold. The reason was his second speech in the Commons which ended on these lines:

> If we believe, as I do, that Scotland as a cultural unity is worth preserving, then we must provide the economic base from which it can go on. I have never thought of myself as a Scottish nationalist, but in the few months that I have been in this House I have been rapidly coming to the conclusion that the only solution is a Scottish government.
>
> *Hansard*, col. 138, 24 July 1961

Those sentiments damned him at the start of his parliamentary life. This was a tragedy both for the party which shunted him aside and for the man himself. We were to discover in John Robertson a man with refined cultural tastes and interests, a passionate Home Ruler with a deep-laid knowledge of economics and the structure of Scottish industry. John was a known right winger, while I was a member of the left-wing Tribune group. A most unlikely pairing. Yet I believe my growing awareness of the justice and need for self-government, and my private enthusiasm to learn economics, rekindled his interest. John let loose in a great flood the concepts and ideas that had been bottled up for years: he was a pleasure to listen to while I was learning.

John and I became close friends. We came from essentially the same working-class background. We both knew the struggle to overcome inadequate basic education, the effort to find the means of self-expression, the agony of uncertainty when knowledge is gained but you are not certain about its value, the hesitancy in speaking out on a subject where you have no previous experience or training in case you blow it and stand exposed. We both knew all about the Scottish working-class lack of self-confidence when confronted by the outward loquacious Englishman of any class; we knew about the Scottish cringe because we were its occasional victims. These shared experiences allowed a political and friendly relationship to develop despite the gap in age and ideology.

We four, Alex, Harry, John and myself, talked frequently about the Scottish dilemma and decided to campaign for a shift in party policy, away from the hard unionist stance and into support for a Scottish Assembly. We did a great deal of quiet lobbying, especially at the 1973 Scottish Labour Conference in Dunoon. We made a special effort to alert journalists to our purpose and sounded out a few influential trade union leaders. Next came the task of setting down our views in pamphlet form. It was not easy because, although we four had much in common, we were not absolutely agreed on what powers a Scottish Assembly should exercise. John Robertson and I undertook the production of the first draft and once the four of us discussed its implications, and identified our differences, he and I produced a final version. We did not rush into print, deciding sensibly to wait until the Kilbrandon Commission on the Constitution had reported, thus enabling us to make swift final adjustments and capitalise on Kilbrandon's support for an assembly. We were fully aware in mid-summer 1973, through good contacts we had with the Commission, that Kilbrandon would favour a directly elected legislative assembly.

40

Our well-laid plan was torpedoed by the death of John Rankin, the Labour MP for the safe seat of Glasgow Govan. A bye-election would be held in late autumn 1973 and we knew that even if Kilbrandon did publish then, we would have to wait until the dust of that bye-election settled. It would have done our cause no good to publish a highly controversial pamphlet as Labour went into fight with its opponents.

The Govan bye-election not only caused a delay in our pamphlet, it also caused a deal of heart-searching on my part, arising from my participation in the Labour campaign. The Labour candidate was Harry Selby. Harry's family and close friends had controlled the Govan constituency Labour Party for years and had sewn up the candidature. Outside of Govan most of the Labour Party was unhappy about the choice. Harry was a revolutionary socialist, firmly entrenched in the 1930s, utterly convinced that his Marxist analysis was an open sesame to understanding the world's problems, that everywhere a titanic struggle was taking place between the boss class and the working class. In a general election Harry would have rolled up the usual big majority but at a bye-election, where candidates are subject to total exposure with every weakness cruelly laid bare to the public, it was a different matter. We all expected a reduced majority but, going up to Govan for the first day of the campaign to canvass, there was no expectation of defeat in my mind.

Margo MacDonald, then the SNP candidate, is now my wife. In those days she was a marginally known opponent. My first encounter with Margo had been a telephone confrontation when I was at the STUC and had blocked her attempt to speak to Paisley Trades Council where she was the SNP parliamentary candidate. That was in 1969. I remember telling my secretary after the phone went down that Margo was able, but cheeky. She was extremely able as events at Govan were to prove.

On my first day I was given canvass cards for Teucherhill, a small housing scheme near to Ibrox park. After two closes I was concerned and at the end of my canvass convinced that we

41

would lose and indeed deserved to lose. I was shattered by the poverty, the people's sense of hopelessness and the appalling housing conditions and surrounding environment. We just didn't have those kind of conditions in the Ayrshire I came from.

Women electors calmly discussed with me the problem of the rats which ran around the closes and backyards and their fear that one would attack the children. "How can I put the baby out in the pram with all those rats about?" was one question that burned into my mind. Another woman took me in for a cup of tea and set out the nature of her family's poverty. Another took me outside to show how, with a huge pool of undrained water covering the whole backyard, she and her neighbours had to walk across a bridge of old bricks. A man pointed to the rubble of broken glass, old cans, and other rubbish in the streets and to a burned-out car lying at the corner. In the very last house I was asked: "Would you vote Labour?" I replied in all honesty that if we were in Ayrshire then I would indeed vote Labour but up here the answer must be no. "That's right," the woman said, "we're all voting for Margo."

It was ridiculous. Here was I a Labour MP, a left winger, canvassing for a left-wing candidate, yet within three hours of starting to campaign the admission was that no one in their right mind would vote Labour! I went back to the committee rooms and spoke briefly to Bunty Urquhart, then assistant Scottish organiser and later a defector to the SDP. Bunty was shrewd and said that this time there were real problems. It was not like Hamilton when Winnie Ewing won in 1967. This went deeper. The SNP had a good candidate but there was a groundswell of opinion that could not be denied or explained simply because of the candidate factor. Bunty agreed that Govan was in a hell of a mess and the Labour Party in the area should be ashamed of itself. Eventually I got hold of Harry Selby, asked him into a quiet corner and expressed my shock and horror at the conditions I had just met in Teucherhill. I suggested it would be a good idea to get the burned-out car cleared away, to which

Harry replied: "I know about that car, we use it to stand on when drumming up support for rent demonstrations." Harry was oblivious to his and the Labour Party's responsibility for the local conditions. It was all the fault of the boss class. I remained in the campaign, doing a couple of public meetings and going with Harry Selby into the docks for trade union meetings, but my heart was not in it.

By polling day only wee Harry was confident of winning. I ended up trudging round the streets near Ibrox Park with Jim Fyfe of the *Glasgow Herald*, a Labour Party member. About 8.00 p.m. we packed it in when Willie Ross toured past us in a car shouting through the loudspeaker system: "Noo's the day and noo's the hour for Govan to kick out Tory power." It was ludicrous. Tories in Govan were a tiny minority; Labour controlled the area and the city of Glasgow. It was Labour power and what was done or not done with it that lay at the heart of the bye-election. Margo won by 571 votes.

The Kilbrandon Commission report, recommending the establishment of a legislative assembly, was published during the bye-election. The report, followed by Margo's victory, changed the face of Scottish politics. Suddenly, the issue of self-government was right up there as first point on the agenda. However, we four were left with a problem. We quickly completed the second part of the pamphlet which was a consideration of Kilbrandon and then our final conclusions in support of an assembly with substantial powers. But it would smack of panic to publish before the Christmas recess, so we decided to wait and bring it out in January, a couple of months before the Scottish conference of the party which was to be held in Ayr in the spring of 1974.

The NUM then intervened, with its second strike confrontation with the Heath government: this ultimately led to election fever sweeping the country immediately after the new year. Heath opted for a February election and it was goodbye to the pamphlet's publication yet again. We did, however, have one consolation. In our view, as we departed Westminster, for a classic class election, there could be no place for the SNP. John Robertson was not so sure but Alex Eadie and Harry Ewing along with myself were sure it was the Tories we had to beat and that the British dimension of the trade union movement versus Tory government would swamp everything else. We failed to realise the message of our own pamphlet. We were wrong. The SNP won seven seats and did well in many others.

The February 1974 election produced a minority Labour government with the certainty of another election in the autumn. The Scottish results of that coming election would determine whether Labour got back with a working majority, but the SNP was clicking Labour's heels north of the border. There was no better time to publish the pamphlet. Alex Eadie had become a Minister in the Department of Energy, but we decided there would be no harm in keeping his name on the cover.

When published, the pamphlet, *Scottish Labour and Devolution*, had a good reception everywhere, except in the Labour Party. The bitterness spilled out at what should have been a victory conference held in Ayr, in March 1974. A devolution motion was debated and defeated amid boos, shouts, personal attacks and pretty poor speeches, including my own. Tam Dalyell had been to the rostrum before me, suggesting that Scottish people were more interested in beer, bingo and football than the great issues which would engage a Scottish Parliament. I lost my temper at the insult on working people and made the worst contribution of my life. There was one good speech, from John Robertson, who was determined to state the democratic case for the Scots handling their own affairs. That night at the civic reception the atmosphere was chill and Willie Ross went out of his way to be woundingly insulting to John Robertson. We left before there was an ugly scene in a mood of black despair.

We stuck to the task, however, and a key man in our efforts was Alex Neil, who had been one of my companions at the Ayr meeting addressed by Winnie Ewing away back in 1967. By

1974 Alex was Labour's Scottish research officer. Another key figure was Bob Brown, previously Scottish correspondent for *The Guardian*, who acted as the party's voluntary unpaid press officer. Alex Neil was talented, enthusiastic and committed to both a left-wing and self-government policy. Bob Brown had been preaching the gospel of Home Rule for years and was one of the main advisers to our small grouping. Alex Neil kept us up to date on all that Ross and the anti-devolutionists were doing to stop any further moves to incorporate a devolution commitment in the party UK manifesto. Bob too had his ear to the ground and, writing under the name of James Alexander, contributed a number of articles to the press at key moments in our continuing campaign.

Those were hectic days. Labour Cabinet Ministers fell over themselves to canvass Scottish views on policy and the decision to place both the headquarters of the British National Oil Corporation and the Offshore Supplies Office in Glasgow came easily. Normally that kind of decision would have taken intensive lobbying but not in those days with another general election looming and the SNP booming in the opinion polls. For the Labour government at that time there was no more important place in the world than our Scotland. Then, in June 1974, Labour's Scottish Executive made its mistake, by rejecting a Scottish Assembly by six votes to five. It was a suicidal decision and the London headquarters of the party then demonstrated what centralism was really all about. They ordered the Scottish Executive to hold a special conference on the issue and then one of the members of the National Executive Committee (NEC), Alex Kitson, went to work to fix the vote in favour of devolution. Alex Kitson was a power in Labour's land both north and south of the border. He was number three in the Transport and General Workers' Union, a member of the party's National Executive Committee and treasurer of the Scottish TUC General Council. Alex believed in a Scottish Parliament and he had the influence to set up a majority trade union block vote at the special conference. We rolled up a number of constituency parties in favour. The conference met in Dalintober Street, Glasgow, on 16 September 1974. It was a mixture of sourness, sincerity and cynicism. With the unions in the bag, the result was 4-1 in favour of an assembly with power.

When the election came in October, Labour's propaganda in Scotland played heavily on the Assembly commitment, with the main election broadsheet describing the coming Labour government as determined to create a "Powerhouse Scotland". The nationalist tide was not turned, merely held at bay, and the nearer we came to polling day the more strident were Labour's efforts to convince the Scots of its genuine intention with regard to devolution. The pressure of the SNP campaign caused a change in the internal policy of Labour's Scottish campaign committee. Alex Neil had told us that at an early stage in planning, Willie Ross, backed by his chief aide Bruce Millan, had an easy time in laying down that under no circumstances was John Mackintosh or myself to play any part in Labour's official campaign, which meant excluding us from press conferences, radio and television programmes and party political broadcasts. It didn't make much difference because a number of Labour MPs, under pressure from the SNP, sought our assistance as supporting speakers in their personal campaigns. I didn't know about John Mackintosh but I was under no illusions knowing I was there to give credibility to colleagues who, only a few months before, were vehement in opposition to an Assembly. The man who printed my election material, and had done for years, John Geddes from Irvine, told me that a number of MPs had come down to his print works, asked to see my election leaflets and had copied them into their own election addresses. I remember John telling me: "They hate your guts, but like your stuff."

Alex Eadie and Harry Ewing had their crosses to bear as well, as did John Robertson whose constituency was next to that of Norman Buchan. Alex and Harry were plagued by a very nervous Tam Dalyell and I even had a couple of phone calls down in Ayrshire from Tam who expressed his concern about

46

the SNP challenge. When members of the Labour Party in later years jeered at me for changing my mind on the issue of an Assembly and independence, I used to think to myself "not as often as some people I could name".

Anxiety was mounting inside the party as we entered the final week of the campaign. That was when John Mackintosh and I received phone calls. We were asked to take leading rôles in the final Scottish opt-out of the television party political broadcast. We were simply asked to come up to Keir Hardie House in Glasgow. We duly arrived, along with the other two participants, Helen Liddell and George Foulkes. There was no script and, when John and I asked what they wanted us to do, we were told to make a broadcast on devolution and, as we knew the policy, just get on with it. So up we all trooped to the BBC.

At the BBC, the Labour Party was represented by a chap from Transport House, Labour's head office in London. He was in charge. It was too late to prepare any detailed script so, at John Mackintosh's suggestion, we went in cold and simply responded to his questions put as the anchor man. The first take was quite good but we decided on another and this came out perfect. However, given the sensitivity of the issue and its importance in the final run-up to polling day, it was not immediately approved for transmission. Our friend from Transport House said he would need to clear the text with London. We then went our separate ways, back to the campaign in our own areas.

Later in the day I received a telephone call from the London fellow, saying it was cleared and that he personally thought it was a brilliant broadcast, just what was needed. After the election Joan Lestor, an NEC member, told me that the Labour Party's private polls showed that our broadcast had a most favourable reception among voters. Key passages from that final "approved" broadcast are worth quoting:

> *John Mackintosh:* In effect we are advocating a directly elected group of Members of Parliament sitting in Edinburgh, who will control Scottish health, housing, education, roads, agriculture,

fisheries; all the matters that are particular and special to Scotland will be under their direct control. And I think it's important too that they will have certain powers of taxation and revenue allocated to them so they can choose what is most important to spend our money on.

*Helen Liddell:* Yes, and it's also very important that they'll have control of the Scottish Development Agency, which the Labour Party has said they will set up. The Scottish Development Agency will be a very powerful economic weapon, designed at bringing jobs to Scotland and it will be primed by North Sea oil so that the benefits of oil go to the ordinary working people of Scotland and build a new economy.

*John Mackintosh:* Jim, could you give an example of what you personally think would be a case where the Scottish Parliament could do something effective and different?

*Jim Sillars:* Well, I think trade and industry are very important elements of the argument for devolution and I think the Scottish Parliament could more easily adapt, and better adapt, United Kingdom policies to suit Scottish circumstances. . . .

The reference to the economic and industrial powers was in line with the Scottish election manifesto which said, on page 16: "We shall therefore give high priority in the next Parliament to the setting up of a Legislative Assembly for Scotland with substantial powers over crucial areas of decision-making." This manifesto commitment followed a major statement of policy, issued by the Labour Party in both London and Glasgow on 5 September 1974, which stated on page 9:

The Scottish and Welsh Assemblies will therefore participate in the decisions of how best to promote their development, for instance by drawing up their own economic plans along the lines set out in "Labour's Programme 1973". *Substantial executive powers in the trade and industry fields* will be transferred from central government, to enable the Assemblies to make decisions in the light of their own needs in the promotion of employment and industrial regeneration. (Emphasis added.)

The election results were good for Labour in Scotland, but the SNP made a big leap forward, taking eleven seats and coming second in a large number of Labour seats. Threatened as never before, my colleagues showed commendable zeal for early action on the Assembly pledge and we were all called to a special meeting in Glasgow on 17 October 1974. It was not so much a meeting as a stampede in the direction of Home Rule. In the press conference held immediately afterwards, the Labour Group made it clear that there would be no "backsliding", emphasising the unity of their commitment and that they expected the body to be operating within about two years. They felt it should become known as "the Scottish Parliament" and that a special Minister should be appointed to get the necessary legislation through. Tam Dalyell (yes Tam Dalyell), the Group chairman, offered the personal view that the Parliament could be working by the autumn of 1976. A Bill to create it would be presented to the Commons in the first session of the new Parliament. Tam went on to add: "Clearly the government and the Labour Party would be brought into disrepute if such a body was created 'with no teeth'." This latter reference to "teeth" was spoken in the context of economic powers. All of these gems are to be found in the *Financial Times* of Friday, 18 October 1974.

Before the following week was over, Harry Ewing had been appointed as Devolution Minister. He joined a Labour government which, because of a poor showing in England, held only a small majority. Wilson was back in Downing Street and, notwithstanding my colleagues' recently discovered passion for an Assembly to be called a Parliament, I was concerned about the future. The admiration I had for Wilson when he was elected leader had given way to contempt and distrust. I was sure he was insincere about devolution and I believed he would try to get rid of me from the Scottish scene by an offer of a junior job in the Department of Environment, looking after the canals of England, or in the Department of Health and Social Security whose Ministers were mainly preoccupied with matters south of the border. I knew my man. I received a phone call from Wilson offering the post of Parliamentary Under-Secretary at the

DHSS. I said no, explaining that social security etc. was not my scene and that I was more interested in economic issues and, of course, the progress of devolution. Wilson said: "So, you won't work with us then?" To which I replied that while I was deeply honoured to be asked into his administration, I still needed to decline. Later, after I left the Labour Party, Wilson felt it necessary to deny that the offer had ever been made. In any event I had given the story to the local newspapers and it got into the nationals. There was no put-down by Wilson then, in the autumn of 1974, and Ross was heard to mutter that it was a bit much to get an offer, turn it down and boast about it. My reason for telling was not to boast. I was trying to strengthen my position as a proponent of devolution and it was important that people inside the movement should know that I could be relied upon to resist the blandishments and bribes held out by the establishment in London.

While John Robertson and I were on the back benches, the other two, Alex Eadie and Harry Ewing, were in the government. Harry's appointment was a key one and we felt that although we faced problems, especially with the Whitehall departments, in the end the Assembly would be established with strong economic powers. That was when I made my first mistake. Alex, Harry and I continued to share the same digs. Knowing that if any serious leaks took place about devolution discussions with government, my link to Harry would raise immediate questions about his reliability, I took a conscious decision never to ask to see his papers, or probe too deeply in our inevitable talk on how things were going. Harry certainly told me about the resistance Ministers were meeting, especially from the Treasury and the Cabinet members with contacts among the North-East group of Labour MPs. But in a phrase he repeated over and over again he would say: "But we have lost no battles yet, Jim." On the other hand my relationship with Alex Eadie was easier in terms of digging for information. Alex's department was Energy and, as I represented a coal-mining area, he would frequently show me his papers, discuss issues in depth and canvass my opinion. If only it had been the other way round.

As the new Parliament settled down, Labour MPs began to regain their nerve, and their unionist leanings. In some parts of the English Labour Party they had, of course, never lost either nerve or anti-devolution sentiment. Tam Dalyell and Robin Cook had a sharp change of mind and came out against an Assembly. Norman Buchan was all things to all men. "Suspended," as Alex Neil once remarked to me, "in a permanent state of indecision." We used to joke that Norman, who had been a member of the Communist Party, would still be hesitating about the wisdom of action two days after the revolution was successful.

After many problems, delays and ambushes by forces inside the civil service and the Parliamentary Labour Party, the day of the White Paper publication drew near. It was to be produced in late autumn 1975. I arranged a special lunch meeting in Glasgow for Harry Ewing and Jim McGrandle who was then the secretary of the party in Scotland. There were just the three of us: the concern of Jim McGrandle and myself was to get a head of steam up in support of the document as soon as it was published. It was a lovely lunch and we engaged mostly in interesting but non-informative chat. Harry talked about the coming White Paper as being good, and about the need to get the party mobilised in a campaign to defend it against the inevitable attacks from the SNP. But he told us nothing about its content.

Harry and I flew back to London after lunch and once I was in my office, Jim McGrandle phoned to ask if I thought he was an idiot. There he was, secretary of the party, shortly to be responsible for running the most important campaign for years and we two had deliberately kept him in the dark. I explained to Jim that I was as mystified as he was, having expected Harry to give us a good briefing. Jim was surprised and then finally convinced when I explained my reasons for not having pressed Harry for detailed information over the year-long debates within the government. I should have been forewarned by that experience but as I said many times in television interviews throughout October 1974 to November 1975, I trusted Harry Ewing. Harry and I agreed that we would break our "no real detailed information" arrangement just prior to the date of publication in November 1975. He would give me the White Paper and his briefing documents. I would take them away, read them and then bring them back. That would give me the same time as the press and television (who received embargoed copies of government publications even before MPs) and so help me handle the inevitable media questions once everything became public.

My office was in the Norman Shaw North building, about three minutes' walk from the Commons where Harry had his office. Passing through the Members' Lobby I got a note to telephone Stewart Maclachlan at the *Daily Record*. I phoned, to hear Stewart's voice ask if I had seen "it". I explained that I was on my way to Harry's to have a look. There was a loud groaning "Oooh" from Stewart, who said it was "terrible" and asked what I was going to do. My reply was that it couldn't be that terrible and anyway I had not read it. With that up I went, then back to the office for over two hours of what proved to be anguished reading. I was stunned. The White Paper set out a scheme for a constitutional skeleton, with no flesh, no muscle, no power and completely pinned down by Westminster. The plug had been pulled on the Powerhouse promised in the election. I read and re-read everything, desperately searching for something substantial which would alter that first devastating impression. There was nothing. It grew worse with each reading and now I understood the cause of Stewart Maclachlan's cry down the phone from Glasgow.

Looking at the White Paper I felt a great sense of shame, in that I had played a part in allowing the Labour Party to use the desires and hopes of the Scottish people to put the party into power, despite the party having little intention of keeping its word. I thought then of my father, who as a typical Scottish working-class Labour voter had freely given his trust and support to the party for a generation. I felt that he and our kind were being treated like dumb oxen. My father could be relied upon to vote Labour and if he swithered even just a little, there would be some promise or other to keep him in line until polling was over and he wouldn't be smart enough to know he was being conned. Scotland was a Labour fiefdom, whose function was to send down its tribute of some forty or more Labour MPs and in return we were to know our place and keep it.

It is difficult at this remove in time, some ten years after the event, to adequately describe how I was torn apart by that White Paper's betrayal of the election pledge. I had believed in the Labour Party. I knew its faults but I believed that at its core lay a wealth of integrity and commitment to the democratic ideal of drawing authority from, and responding to, the people. As the scales fell from my eyes, the full extent of Harold Wilson's politically corrupting influence on the party became clear. I saw that a once great liberalising institution had become a cynical outfit, whose English majority dictated events, and whose Scottish acolytes were more interested in position than in transforming society within Scotland.

I took the White Paper back to Harry, telling him bluntly that it was a disgrace and that, bearing in mind his claims never to have lost a battle, I could only conclude that was because he had never fought one within the government. He claimed the White Paper would be popular. We parted with me telling him that I would oppose it and that I didn't care if I was the only one. I, for one, knew a betrayal of Scotland's needs when it was staring me in the face.

Within forty-eight hours the official launch of the White Paper took place. I flew up to Glasgow to take part, with Harry, in a BBC television programme examining the White Paper. As we met in the studios Harry said he hoped I had changed my mind because he and Willie Ross had received a good reception from the Scottish press earlier that day. "Then they are as wrong as you are," was my reply. I had no idea that every newspaper was even then writing the most stinging criticisms of Harry's pride and joy. There was widespread anger throughout Scotland at the failure of the proposed Assembly to live up to expectations. For me the end came on the second and third of December 1975. On the evening of the second, the Scottish Labour Group met and, when confronted with their manifesto, the party's statement of 5 September 1974 and the text of the party political broadcast on 4 October 1974, their position was summed up by Hugh Brown, MP for Provan, who told me that he was not going to be bound by "these wee bits of paper". Norman Buchan claimed that the party had given no commitments to economic power. By a crushing majority, the Scottish Labour Group backed the White Paper.

The next day, 3 December, the full Parliamentary Labour Party met. It was to see Norman Buchan in a typical pose. He had now changed his mind from the previous evening. Yes, the party had given the commitments as charged by John Robertson and myself but these had all been honoured in the White Paper. The English Labour MPs were delighted by the Scottish Group's retreat. I was in despair because I saw no prospect of my Scottish colleagues forcing the English MPs into the kind of action that would guarantee an Assembly with powers.

The following weekend I had a private meeting in Ayr with Bob Brown and Alex Neil when we decided that as things stood, given the attitudes I have just described, there was no chance of an Assembly from Labour unless they were pushed to the wall. We decided the best thing was to quit and flush Labour's betrayal into the open.

*Chapter 3*

# TOWARDS THE SNP

ON 10 DECEMBER 1975 I resigned from both the Scottish Executive and the Scottish Labour Group. I wrote a long letter to my own agent, Jim Tanner, and gave him the following explanation:

> There is a need to explain further to you my reasons for this step. I am sick at heart and in the depth of despair because of the twisting and turning and cynicism shown by my Labour colleagues with regard to the matter of our pledge to the people on the powers and status of the Assembly.
>
> You know from your own experience that our election material was lifted, in both February and October elections, by a number of Labour candidates who are now MPs. You know the demands that were made for me to be used as a speaker and instrument for devolutionary endorsement, for various candidates during both elections, especially the October one.
>
> What sickens me is that the twisting and turning betrays a fact: we in the Labour Party were insincere in the promises we made. The experience I went through on Tuesday night, 2 December, when Labour MPs were dismissing our documents and statements as "wee bits of paper", shows that the worst feature of our performance is that we believe the people are stupid enough to believe anything and so we can say anything and get out of it later.
>
> I value idealism and integrity in politics. I know that idealism must be tempered by what is practicable when we come to formulate policies prior to elections but once made the integrity of an election pledge must be inviolate. That is patently not the case with the Assembly, a matter I regard as of the utmost importance.

All through this past summer I was constantly told that the White Paper would be all right. I knew it would never go as far on powers as I would have liked, but that was not important. What was important was the understanding given to me that it would meet the election commitment and could, therefore, be presented with honour. No one can complain if the government went no further than its election commitment.

As you know I was anxious to help launch a campaign in favour of the White Paper and spent some time and a number of speeches during the summer trying to prepare common ground for the party to unite on and fight on. All this on the understanding that the White Paper was OK.

Had I known the extent of the roll back I would have made the strongest representations with the government, privately but forcefully and indeed fiercely, for the defects to be attended to. However, I knew next to nothing and was completely unprepared for what was there when I read the thing two days before publication.

I have tried not to get the Assembly issue out of perspective. There are other things of importance. But I believe this issue transcends all else in its importance to the people we claim to represent. If their needs are to be met, especially in the industrial and job sector of activity, we must have substantial powers vested in the Assembly. I believe now that what might have been acceptable two years ago is no longer on and will need to be vastly improved upon. How that is to be achieved is something I am struggling with now.

If you will set adequate time aside I shall make a personal and prepared statement at the next meeting of the CLP, setting out my position and whatever course of action I believe I should take. I doubt if I am likely to be the most popular man in the room on the 20th December.

I am sorry to burden you with this long letter. A Labour agent's life is grim enough without having an MP who is always in trouble, or making trouble as my colleagues would put it. I wish my rôle in the party could have been otherwise, but that apparently is not to be.

You have been extremely kind and helpful to me throughout the past six years, hence the length and frankness of this letter. You more than anyone are entitled to a full explanation.

At the South Ayrshire constituency party meeting on 20 December, I told the members I was leaving and would fight the next election as a Scottish Labour Party candidate. All of us were in a distraught condition. We had been close and good friends for years and I told everyone that my strictures on the Labour Party did not embrace them. I did warn, however, that if party members went along with what was happening then they would kill for all time the idealism that had so marked out the Labour Party and would leave the way open for the rise of careerists such as George Robertson and Bruce Millan.

There was nothing premeditated about the decision to form a Scottish Labour Party (SLP). When we decided to break we did not even have a name for the new organisation. It was Neal Ascherson who suggested the final choice. Many in the Labour Party made out that we had a deep-laid plot. Far from careful planning, our action was an emotional response born of disgust. There was no preparation, no attempt to create an organisation ahead of break time, no effort at all to suborn the South Ayrshire constituency party and thus establish quickly a safe and stable base from which to operate. Our intentions were pure, but in timing, strategy and tactics we did everything wrong.

It was a typical Scottish rush downhill with the blood flooding the head, drowning all cool appraisal. John Robertson who made the most masterly summing up of the White Paper on its publication day, "the Assembly is more closely caged than a lion at the zoo", joined us in the dash downhill after some hesitation. His position prior to his final decision to join was eloquently summed up in a public statement from him on 16 December 1975:

> If the Labour Party in Scotland accepts what is being done then I too will be faced with what will be for me, very grave decisions. The loyalties and hopes of a lifetime are not to be discarded easily or lightly, indeed that piece of surgery is likely to have fatal results.
>
> I am not yet without hope but time is running out. What gesture I can make to political honesty will not disturb the still waters of the Scottish Labour Party, yet however modest my contribution may be I have to make peace with myself and I find the need for decision very pressing.

C

When we called the inaugural meeting of the SLP, in early January 1976, we were no better prepared for the launch than we had been for the break. We had no draft constitution and no guidelines setting out the basis on which people were asked to join. We made no attempt to screen those who came to the meeting and the organising committee elected at the meeting came genuinely from the body of the kirk. We had not even foreseen the arrival of the International Marxist Group (IMG) and they were in our midst from the start, and were ultimately the force that destroyed us.

It may seem remarkable that two MPs, both with safe seats and some considerable experience in the organised trade union movement, and Alex Neil with a brilliant career ahead of him, should take such an ill-prepared leap in the dark. A political judgement would be that we were foolish and almost inevitably bound to fail. We were guilty of not acting and thinking as self-interested politicians and we should have done what the SDP founding group did years later — taken more time to lay the groundwork, organisation and base of our new party. We acted from principle and did not stop to scheme and plot. Of course, we knew the chances against success were slim. Alex Neil, Bob Brown and myself, together with John Robertson, knew how the Labour Party would deal with anyone who left it but we believed that someone somewhere along the line had to take a stand, and take risks.

On leaving the Labour Party I had a meeting with Bob Mellish, Chief Whip of the PLP, who told me bluntly that I was wasting a great career over nothing. He forecast that there would not be an Assembly: his English members just would not have it. I should accept the reality. I offered Bob a bye-election, provided there were certain conditions. These were that he would give me a written undertaking that the labour Party would move the writ for the bye-election exactly four weeks after my resignation from Parliament and that we would make the deal public. My reasons for this were that I knew if left to itself, the Labour Party, as it had done when Dick Taverne left over the EEC, would delay the writ for as long as possible hoping that the issue would have died down in a few months' time and also so that the resigning MP could be blamed for leaving the constituency unrepresented. Mellish told me he didn't want a bye-election. I should have got that in writing but did not. Later, in the 1979 General Election, Mellish made a damaging statement that I should have resigned in 1976 and that I never offered him a bye-election. It was ironic when, some years later, Mellish himself left the Labour Party and accused it, and it him, of the most devilish political malpractices. Fortunately for my own reputation the matter of the bye-election was raised with me in public at a press conference. *The Scotsman* of 9 February 1976 records:

> Mr Jim Sillars, the first MP to join the Scottish Labour Party, said yesterday that he was prepared to fight a bye-election for his South Ayrshire parliamentary seat. "The Cabinet just need to request me to have a bye-election," he said.

Before that small digression, I was emphasising our act of principle. There were two issues of major importance for us. One was the Labour Party's denial of any real commitment to the election pledges made in order to secure Scottish votes and thus ensure the return of a Labour government. The second was that without a Scottish Assembly with powers in the industrial field Scotland would be unable to withstand the dual centralist pressures of the United Kingdom and EEC. We were living in a group of capitalist economies where, given their remit to increase the value and subsequently a return from capital stock, institutional investors were bound to see the South East of England and the golden triangle of Europe as far more lucrative investment territory than Scotland which lies far from major markets. Our Scotland lies on the periphery of industrial Europe and the disadvantage we suffer in the market place can only be balanced with the political weight of an Assembly which had power to pursue policies suited to our scale and abilities.

Given our non-existent preparations and the ravages wrought

by the destructive forces of the IMG in our ranks, the SLP did not succeed. It is not my intention to delve into all the reasons for our electoral failure because, however harrowing, sobering and maturing the experience was, it was not the electoral effort but the policy-making we attempted within the new party that was decisively influential. It should be remembered that the SLP was formed by people in favour of maximum devolution. Some of us had looked into the issue of independence, especially within the context of the EEC, but all of us would have settled for something really substantial in a UK context. As an independent party we faced the need for policies, the need to spell out in detail just how we would tackle the economic, social and foreign policy issues facing Scotland. It was a remarkable experience to step outside the womb of the Labour Party. On one hand it was traumatic. Willie Ross remarked that there was a special kind of hell for people like us and was correct. It meant wrenching up one's roots, walking away from the warm comfortable atmosphere of a big organisation geared to mutual support, being in direct opposition to lifelong friends, tormented by the feelings of being a traitor, the soul crushed by the emotional agony of viewing as worthless all that only a few months before you had regarded as good. On the other hand, escaping from the party's taboos and the limitations on thought imposed by trying to fit into what the English majority would accept, the intellect became free to roam, question, probe and consider all options on every issue.

But the overwhelming influence was trauma at leaving. I carried a heavy and permanent burden of sadness at the need to break with the Labour Party. It was years before I was to be free of that feeling but looking back it was the right thing to do. I no longer believed that Labour would create fundamental changes for the better in the life of Scotland's working people. The idealism that fuelled the early movement was spent. The Labour Party's commitment to real change was restricted to its rhetoric and the era of opportunists and careerists was upon us. It was really no place for me.

Despite our ultimate failure and the debilitating effect of the International Marxist Group constantly burrowing away into the foundations of our new party, we were a happy band in the SLP. There are too many people to name but none will grudge a word about Litster Gardiner who eventually became the party's secretary. A Scot trained in English law, his practice lay across the border just south of Carlisle. None attended more meetings in Scotland than he: he was capable of the most prodigious administrative and campaigning efforts. He was the pillar we all leaned on when things got rough; he was a source of encouragement in our policy-making efforts.

We started those efforts by producing a statement, *Jobs and Industry*, which was chiefly the work of Alex Neil. As first one draft and then another was examined, we began to see the serious limitations which continued membership of the United Kingdom would bring. Joe Farrell, who ultimately became Executive Chairman of the party, argued that we had to accept the reality of the EEC dimension in Scottish political and industrial life. This matter of the EEC was not new to John Robertson and myself for we had examined it before. In a debate on devolution on 4 February 1975, when the thought of leaving the Labour Party would have seemed impossible, I said this:

> . . . if we are locked inside the EEC I would not argue that Scotland should come out. That is, perhaps, some comfort to my hon. Friend the Member for West Lothian. I believe that we should retain our close links with the other people inside the British Isles but I would certainly argue that it would then be in the interests of the Scottish people to have direct nation-State membership of the Community. If we were foolish enough to continue inside the EEC it might be time to write a new verse to an old song.
>
> *Hansard*, col. 1216

As with industrial policy, so it was on defence, foreign policy and trade. We were a separate Scottish Labour Party and quite naturally sought a constitutional framework in which our separate and independent thoughts on policy could be advocated with some eventual chance of implementation. But, within the United Kingdom set-up, we had no "national" base, merely a sub-national area in which to work. We wanted no nuclear bases on Scottish soil but how could that be achieved when, short of independence, the final decision lay with the English majority?

And so it went on with each policy examination pushing us further and further along the road to an independence position, always against the background of Joe Farrell's tireless projection of the EEC dimension. By October 1976 a working party, under Joe's chairmanship, produced our definitive position on Scottish government. This was presented on 9 October, and noted in its opening paragraph: "The European dimension *requires* Scottish autonomy." We also had to struggle with a socialist and working-class dilemma. We had broken with the British Labour Party and felt bitter and resentful about the rôle of English Labour MPs in sabotaging efforts for a Scottish Assembly. But we were not revengeful. We did not think that Scots could be part of a state for over 270 years (during which time the working people had constructed a great movement and achieved much by joint effort) and then leave the Union without any regard for the well-being of those who had been our comrades in the warmest sense of the word. This dilemma was particularly marked on the issue of oil policy. The SNP were quite open about saying it was Scottish oil. While we did not dispute the geographical reality behind that statement, nor the right of the Scots to their own resources, we felt it unwise and immoral to take a purely Scottish decision on the oil question without regard to the grave consequences the loss of the oil facility would have for the English economy and the English people. We regarded Westminster's conduct in denying Scotland any rights in oil as immoral too. In our view the sensible policy was to share the resource between the two nations by special treaty. An oil-sharing policy covering those areas already licensed for exploration and exploitation would give Scotland an abundance of new capital resources without causing severe difficulties to the English position which would become fatal if international financial people thought that the English economy was to be removed from the life-giving drip feed from oil. The SLP believed that an oil-sharing policy was a civilised and prudent way for two partners to deal with a vital asset upon their divorce. I still believe that is the case.

All this time the devolution drama was continuing in Westminster. The government had been forced by public demand to alter some of the provisions of the ill-starred White Paper. Eventually there came a Bill, far from the election promise, but a Bill. We believed the formation of the SLP, with Labour threatened from the Left in Scotland for the first time, had shifted the government. It did not shift the English Labour MPs, nor the virulent opposition of the Welshman who is anglicised in all but accent, Neil Kinnock. With Cabinet Ministers playing a dirty game of encouraging rebels to fight their own government's Bill by filibuster, a guillotine became necessary in order to force the measure through. The guillotine motion fell because the government could not carry its own MPs and because, notwithstanding his consistent advocacy of Home Rule, David Steel led the Liberals into the lobby to bring the Bill to an end. The Devolution Bill was introduced in December 1976; the guillotine motion was lost on 22 February 1977, with twenty-two Labour MPs voting against and twenty-three abstaining. Steel saw that a defeat for the government would precipitate a political crisis. Labour's small majority had disappeared and they were now relying upon the support of the minority parties. Steel threw away Home Rule for the Lib-Lab pact, as his first step in his attempts to realign United Kingdom politics. Scottish need took second place to his plans for south of the border. Of course, Steel dressed up this betrayal of a long-standing Liberal policy by pretending that Liberal influence would be decisive in getting a better second Bill. When the second Bill was published, there was little material difference between it and the first attempt. More important, when the crucial issue of the referendum and the 40 per cent rule arose, there was no Liberal veto on the Labour Party. The pass was sold again.

Eventually the Scotland Bill passed with the infamous 40 per cent rule, that 40 per cent of the electorate had to vote "Yes", laid within its provisions as a self-destruct mechanism. The hypocrites who pushed that rule into the Bill claimed that such a great constitutional change as devolution required a threshold of support. Yet, in the EEC referendum of 1975, they said a simple majority of those voting was enough although that issue involved the transfer of sovereignty. Devolution, properly defined, as it was by Enoch Powell, meant sovereignty retained at Westminster. The 40 per cent rule was an enormous psychological burden on the Yes campaigners. By employing a crooked referendum to prevent Scotland forming its own directly elected assembly, the United Kingdom Parliament debauched the democratic ideal. They made a set of rules designed to make the Scots poke a finger in their own eye and one lesson I learned was that the UK Parliament can never be trusted again to engage in honest dealing with Scotland.

When it came to the referendum, we saw Scotland fatally split. John Mackintosh had been the moving power in setting up the Yes for Scotland campaign as an all-party effort but he died in the prime of life before the campaign really got underway. This was a crippling blow. As well as losing John's eloquence and influence, his death narrowed our base. We had plenty of Conservatives, Liberals, Labour people, Nationalists, SLP members and people without party affiliation. But few were widely known to the media and the public. With John gone, we were left with SLP and SNP Members of Parliament as the front people, along with Margo MacDonald, also clearly identified as SNP. Without John Mackintosh pushing and pulling, we had little chance of getting other MPs from other parties to join thus giving us the wide base needed. It was chicken and egg. People like Alick Buchanan Smith, Tory MP for Angus and Mearns, and Russell Johnston, Liberal MP for Inverness, claimed we had too narrow a base for them to join. But, unless they joined, we could not widen our base.

Knowing that my presence meant that no Labour MP would join, I tried to leave the Yes for Scotland campaign quietly. I made a suggestion to the campaign committee that I should stand down and let Alick Buchanan Smith take over, restricting myself to a series of arranged debates with Tam Dalyell. This offer was accepted, with our two Tory joint secretaries in agreement. They were unknown nationally at that time but Ian Hoy is now a Tory regional councillor in Lothian and Paul Martin leads the Tory Group on Edinburgh District Council. The man asked to convey this suggestion to Alick was another Tory, Tim Noble. The suggestion was refused by Alick. So, we remained stuck. If I resigned in public, opponents would say the Yes side was falling apart. We all agreed to soldier on but it was not a good sign.

Meanwhile, there were bigger problems coming from the Labour Party. They issued a decision on 27 January 1978 to have no truck with any other party or group, except the STUC and the Co-operative Party. Helen Liddell, Labour's Scottish Secretary, showed her harsh sectarian attitude at a press conference when she remarked: "We will not be soiling our hands by joining any umbrella Yes group. We will be fighting for devolution only with the Scottish TUC and the Co-operative Party." That would have been bad enough but Labour were actually playing a double game. Officially it was in favour of a Yes vote but many MPs and leading activists, such as Brian Wilson, and constituency parties, were campaigning on the No side. Tam Dalyell MP and Robin Cook MP were two of the most fervent anti-Assembly Labour campaigners. This meant that Labour's official campaign stuttered and spluttered, gave no positive leadership and thus further weakened Scottish resolve. In fact, there were frequent occasions when SNP and SLP activists in the Yes for Scotland campaign quietly helped out the very small groups of Labour Yes activisits by distributing thousands of official Labour leaflets.

For me, the person epitomising the Labour Party campaign of those crucial days, was that self-proclaimed hero of Scottish culture, a man who frequently claimed in House of Commons speeches that he had yearned to see a Scottish legislature all his life, Norman Buchan. When the bugle sounded he went AWOL. During the campaign, when the *Sunday Mail* on 14th January 1979 asked every Scottish MP how he would vote, Buchan chickened out, declaring "That is a secret". There has rarely been so open a display of political cowardice.

There is no doubt that a Labour Party that could so astutely ride two horses in different directions simultaneously was a formidable outfit. But its tactics during the Referendum, and after, reinforced the conviction of those like myself that it had become nothing but a self-serving power-grabbing machine, quite without principle or deep concern about anything except its own institutional advancement. The people came a poor second.

The whole Referendum was a nightmare for me. By then I was seriously ill with a stomach ulcer, being warned by my doctor that if I did not slow down there would be a bye-election in South Ayrshire. But with Alick Buchanan Smith's refusal to step in when I stepped down, there was no alternative but to continue the campaigning effort. The first worry was money. Yes for Scotland did not have any and I had to fund the first print of our first leaflet, hoping it would sell well enough to pay me back and finance the next printing. It did sell and we finally printed and paid for one million. But it was an uphill struggle even when some individuals made, for them, quite substantial contributions. But we needed that money to cover telephones and the printing of other leaflets. It was a shoestring organisation, kept going by the sheer dedication of the many young people who worked themselves into the ground trying to match the well-financed, well-oiled No campaign. There was no money to help those of us who were travelling the country in the most appalling winter for years. My personal debt mounted and it was a terrible psychological burden to cart around.

I mentioned the weather. There was deep snow and ice covering the whole of Scotland. It was also the trade union winter of discontent, with little or no snow clearing on the roads: the whole of Lothian Region had ungritted sheets of icy roads for weeks on end. The car journey from Glasgow to Edinburgh took two-and-a-half hours — I can recall travelling by car from Glasgow to Dumfries in the teeth of a blizzard with the A74 road disappearing before my weary eyes. After reaching Dumfries, where I spoke at a meeting, I faced a three-hour drive, slipping and sliding, back to Ayr, a journey that normally took only eighty minutes.

The misery for me was increased one Saturday evening when I spoke at a meeting in Lanark, chaired by Tom McAlpine of the SNP. It was well attended and went on for a long time. About ten minutes before the end I felt the nausea welling up, a sure sign of vomiting to come. I got out of the meeting just in time, upsetting one or two people by the brusque way I turned down invitations to linger for a coffee and a chat, got into my car, made it to the edge of town and there in private up came the blood. I was in a dreadful state and it took over two hours of driving, stopping, vomiting to get back to my home in Annbank, just outside of Ayr. By then I was covered in blood, needing a bath and bed. My neighbour's light was on. The kind soul had waited up to tell me that there was no water supply. The pipe, serving our row of country cottages, had burst. We were in the NUPE strike area and there would be no repair. I lived on my own and this was a personal disaster.

For six or seven weeks I fought the campaign from a freezing house with no water. My neighbours in the cottages and farms around became irate constituents, demanding that their MP do something. I could not. I supported the strike against the government's 5 per cent wage norm. My biggest problem was a retired RAF officer who phoned me frequently with hysterical threats against the union pickets preventing work being done on the burst pipe. This military type kept threatening to drive the pickets away with a gun he had for shooting game. And so it went on, week after week, utter misery for everyone.

Throughout the campaign we could feel the Scottish people wilting and swithering. The Yes side was seriously divided. The No side was united and hammered away with messages of fear about separation, the loss of jobs and the loss of subsidies. George Cunningham, the MP who fathered the 40 per cent rule, came north to his native land. He sat for an Islington seat — one of what Willie Ross named the "Sudetan Scots". Outside the gates of Govan Shipbuilders, he threatened the men that a Yes vote would see their subsidies removed with the inevitability of closure.

Business interests said devolution would lead to the ruin of the Scottish economy. Nicholas Fairbairn claimed on television that a devolved Scotland would be led by wild men and women, citing Jimmy Reid, Margo MacDonald and myself as examples of that breed. The No side had limitless finance and used it effectively.

On the weekend before polling we were losing and a special meeting of Yes for Scotland people was held in Margo Mac-Donald's house in East Kilbride. A key man was Donald Bain. He had been SNP research officer but had by then gone to work in Europe. He came back for the final phase of the campaign and put up £1,000. With the necessary finance secured, we had a long debate which finally settled our strategy, tactics and publicity for the last desperate four days. We knew the 40 per cent hurdle would not be cleared. Equally, we knew we must get a Yes vote if there was to be any short-term hope of pushing the Labour government into creating the Assembly and any long-term hope of reviving the demand for self-government. By however narrow a margin we had to be in front of the No vote.

Polling was on 1 March 1979, with the results announced the next day. It was a close thing, a narrow victory for Yes. In my view that last four final days of effort just pulled us in front. The actual vote was:

| Yes | 1,230,937 |
|-----|-----------|
| No  | 1,153,502 |

It was a bitter disappointment but it was a win which, if those in the self-government movement had the nerve, could be used for the benefit of Scotland. It was still possible to achieve the Assembly.

The result of the Referendum placed the Labour government in dire straits. The Lib-Lab pact had ended. Its fortunes were at a low ebb and it desperately needed time in which to sort out the fiasco of the pay-policy collapse and give the public a period in which to forget the rigours and horrors of the winter. The Tories were moving in for the kill, knowing that Labour's options and its ability to keep the minority groups dangling in support had narrowed.

Tory joy and expectation of Labour's impending defeat burst out when their hero entered the chamber of the House of Commons on the first parliamentary day following the Referendum. There was a great ovation for Tam Dalyell, seen by the Tories as having dealt a fatal blow to his own government as a leader of the No campaign. But all was by no means lost. The government had to table a motion to repeal the Scotland Act because the Yes vote did not pass the 40 per cent barrier. That was the law and the government could not avoid it. However, there was nothing to prevent the government tabling the repeal order, and then voting against it, thus saving the Scotland Act and the Assembly. With the repeal order defeated, the government could then go on to lay the orders setting the date for Assembly elections and irrevocable steps would have been taken to set up the Assembly. Labour could have said: "We are forced by law to set this repeal order before the House, but we also have an election commitment to set up a Scottish Assembly and, given that the Yes side had a majority, we are going to honour our pledge. We shall do this by laying a three-line whip on Labour MPs to vote down the order and that three-line whip will be taken as a vote of confidence among our own members."

Labour was a minority government but, on the question of devolution for Scotland, it could command a substantial majority in the Commons. The following shows the voting strengths in the lobby at that time:

| | |
|---|---:|
| Labour | 307 |
| Conservative | 282 |
| Liberal | 14 |
| SNP | 11 |
| SLP | 2 |
| Plaid Cymru | 3 |
| Ulster Unionists and allies | 10 |
| Others (Irish) | 2 |

If Labour had tabled the repeal order, then invited the House to vote it down, it would have commanded a majority of at least 31: 45 of a majority if the Liberals voted rather than abstain. The Liberal Scottish Conference, 16 March 1979, voted to implement the Scotland Act, so the Liberals in Parliament were unlikely to vote against the government. Even if they did, the majority would have been 17, as the Irish intended to abstain anyway. Once voted down, the repeal order could not be brought forward again. The Scotland Act would be safe. Efforts to get a united Scottish demand for government action along these lines failed very quickly. Labour devolutionists threw in the towel and proved useless in the crisis. That meant a great deal resting upon the sagacity of the SNP.

Strenuous efforts were made to establish a dialogue between the government and the SNP. John Robertson and I talked to people on both sides in an effort to define possible areas of disagreement and agreement. In the House of Commons the government leg-man was Deputy Chief Whip Walter Harrison. Operating out of Downing Street was Roger Stott, the Prime Minister's Parliamentary Private Secretary, who tried to get a line through to the SNP Executive in Scotland via Margo MacDonald. Another regular caller on Margo's phone was John Smith, then in the Cabinet. The SNP Executive did agree by a majority that the government should not be brought down on a vote of confidence but by then the Executive's influence on the

SNP parliamentary group was non-existent. Everything depended upon the parliamentary group in the House of Commons.

It was an unfolding tragedy. Hamish Watt, the SNP whip, knew how much depended upon the coming vote of confidence which the Tories were tabling. He wanted to offer the government a deal. In return for Labour using a three-line whip to vote down the repeal order, the SNP would guarantee to support the government for the remaining seven months of its life, always provided the dates were irrevocably set for the Assembly elections. Hamish knew this was the only chance of saving the Assembly. He also realised the enormous damage to Scottish self-confidence that the Referendum result had imposed. The Labour government needed time to regroup after the winter of discontent but the SNP needed time to help restore the spirit within the Scots, without which the SNP could not hold at the coming election.

Hamish Watt actually arranged a meeting between Callaghan and Donald Stewart, the SNP parliamentary group leader. But Stewart refused to be present as Gordon Wilson insisted on his non-attendance. The SNP Group split by seven votes to four in favour of bringing down the government but George Reid and Hamish Watt were sorely tempted to break ranks and keep Labour in office. Donald Stewart put George Reid under great pressure and it was with extreme reluctance that George followed the group line. Hamish remained stubborn. He was threatened with expulsion from both the group and the party and right to the very last hours he sought a way out of voting Labour into opposition and the SNP into limbo. As he told me years later, while sitting in misery during the censure debate, he was deeply stung by Jim Callaghan's famous crack that the SNP's decision to vote down the government and precipitate an early election was the first time turkeys had voted for an early Christmas.

With the SNP successfully boxing itself in, it all lay in the hands of the Labour Party — specifically that part bitterly opposed to devolution. If the SNP was unhinged, I found significant numbers of Labour MPs in the grip of a death wish. Despite leaving the party, I had remained on good personal terms with old friends like Dennis Skinner, Eric Heffer and Neil Kinnock. It was still possible to put the SNP into a position where it must support the government or at least make it possible for George Reid and Hamish Watt to either vote against their party's whip or abstain and thus save the government. But for that to happen, Labour would have to declare that it would deliver a vote against the repeal order on a three-line whip. I set about seeing if that was possible, contacting my three friends who were all important figures on the anti-devolution side of the PLP and a number of others. Skinner was non-commital, although he felt that nothing could be done to prevent the inevitable carrying of the Tory vote of no confidence. Next, I got hold of Neil Kinnock and Eric Heffer at the bar of the House where, for some time, I tried to persuade them to push their weight behind the kind of action that would make the SNP support the government or at least abstain.

My case was simple. Labour was bound to lose an early election. They agreed but Neil put an end to the discussion with words that stuck with me all through the weeks to come when Labour canvassers were hammering the SNP for having brought down the government. When faced with the argument about defeat for Labour at an early election, Neil replied, "So be it then." And so it was. Eric took the same line and others I talked to were already drafting their election addresses. *The real question at the end of the day, even allowing for the poor tactical performance of the SNP, was whether the Labour MPs from England and some from Wales would put the life of their government before their hatred for a Scottish Assembly.* Walter Harrison did not stop trying. There was a final meeting of Labour whips, after a canvass of opinion among the various regional groups, to see whether Callaghan could risk putting devolution to the test of a three-line whip. The meeting decided against. They thought their MPs would bring down their own government rather than concede an Assembly. It was better that the odium attached to bringing down the government should fall on some other suckers.

When the vote of confidence debate was wound up by the Prime Minister, he could only go as far as to say that the matter of voting on the repeal order would be brought to a conclusion at an early date. There was no set date and no promise of him making it a three-line whip. The SNP, foolishly in my view, then and now, voted against the government and it fell by one vote. A few hours before the vote I met Hamish Watt, SNP MP for Banff. He was a picture of misery. He knew it was a mistake to vote against the government but his group had decided against his advice. Had the SNP adopted the Watt line and held on until Callaghan brought forward the repeal motion, then either the Assembly would have been saved (unlikely, I agree) or Labour MPs would have been clearly seen as the people who killed it. All the SNP did was to take the blame for sinking the Labour government and save the Labour MPs from total exposure.

The day after the vote Callaghan called the General Election, I took all the files from my office, piled them into my car, and drove north. I knew I was not coming back. Indeed, I did not want to come back. I knew the fatal wound that had been inflicted upon the Scottish cause by the Referendum and that Thatcher would win and thus change the order of the whole political agenda. Besides, I was ill, in heavy debt through meeting every penny of my own political and referendum costs, tired and exhausted.

Back in South Ayrshire, I was supported by a great group of people. If I tried to mention everyone I would leave some- one out inadvertently. So I will stick, on names, to the two men who were my personal assistants throughout the campaign and to my election agent and his wife. The South Ayrshire SLP members had come with me into the new party, without being asked, and stuck loyally by me through thick and thin. Despite the waves of hostility that lapped around them in Labour South

73

Ayrshire, they were adamant in their beliefs, unafraid to stand their ground down the pit, in the shops, at the bowling green, or on the streets. Nothing was too much trouble and, by dint of extremely hard work, they had put together enough cash to fight a good campaign. My election agent was Bill McCrorie, ably assisted by his wife Isobel. My two personal assistants were Willie Grant from Dalrymple and Billy Sproat from Patna. Bill and Isobel took on the huge task of organising the campaign and Willie Grant and Billy Sproat would pick me up at 9 a.m. each day and deposit me at home around 11 p.m. Despite our problems we had a happy campaign.

I could not tell anyone, except Alex Neil and Bob Brown, that we were not going to win. I knew it would be close but the implacable hostility of the NUM, even going as far as to pay for a most expensive advertisement in the *Daily Record* in order to lambast me, would tell in the end. Isobel McCrorie had sharp political instincts, and fairly early on she spotted the possibility of defeat. But she kept the feeling to herself.

Exhausted as I was, I was strangely happy within myself. The Labour Party was vicious and my son Matthew was hounded out of New Cumnock by a stream of highly personalised venom directed at his father. But I had grown used to slander and crude behaviour and felt sorry that people for whom I had great respect should so demean themselves.

The SLP fought a fine socialist campaign in South Ayrshire and much that we said has proved highly relevant both in respect of the communities in the constituency and Scotland as a whole. We warned about the consequences of defeating the self-government movement, the intellectual crisis in the socialist movement, the danger that would flow from a Thatcher government without an effective Scottish opposition and the need to fight back immediately from the Referendum setback. We did well in difficult circumstances but we lost, as I expected. After the count I pointed out to the victorious Labour supporters that we in Scotland still had not resolved the paradox of rejoicing in Labour winning in our country, while the English were voting in a Tory government. Sam Purdie spoke again. Whether it was to any avail time alone will tell.

I have one abiding memory of that election campaign. A contribution made from the floor by a very old retired miner, at a public meeting in Netherthird, Cumnock. I never knew his name. He asked if, instead of putting a question, he could say something: that was normal in our area, so the chairman let him go. We expected criticism and maybe a lecture about staying in the Labour Party. I took down what he said, which was this:

> Before I was born my father was involved in socialist politics and from boyhood I have known all the great men — Hardie, Maxton, Tom Johnston and Wheatley. I have heard some describe the wonderful society that socialism will bring to the working class.
>
> All of them went down to the Parliament in London, and from there they could never deliver socialism to the Scottish working class. It is only when our people realises that all of our socialist dreams have been destroyed by the London connection that we will make any progress. We need a Parliament of our own. That's our only hope.

I kept that note in my files. He spoke to the lesson I had learned during my time in the House of Commons. We cannot have socialism for Scotland without self-government. Despite my defeat, that was the lesson still drumming in my head as I left South Ayrshire.

The election of 1979 was a disaster for the SNP with only Donald Stewart and Gordon Wilson retaining their seats: it was annihilation for the SLP. Some people did try to keep the party going but my personal life now had to take priority. It was the same with Alex Neil, whose health too was bad and who was in even deeper financial water than myself. He had made enormous personal sacrifices and all of us advised him to set politics aside for a while.

After the election I had a period of unemployment and found great difficulty getting a job. Finally, I was lucky, being appointed Director of the Scottish Federation of Housing

Associations, which necessitated a move to Edinburgh. It was a wrench leaving my home county and South Ayrshire, which I loved. I felt no bitterness towards the people, only sorrow, because I knew whatever personal problems I was having, they were nothing in comparison to what an English Tory government would create in a defenceless Scotland and a prostrate South Ayrshire. Long before the Referendum I had heard John Mackintosh, Labour MP for Berwick and East Lothian, warn that if after more than a decade of shouting and demanding an Assembly, the Scots failed to grasp their chance, then we would never be taken seriously again, and would be defenceless. I knew he was going to be proved correct yet again, dead and gone though he was.

During the autumn of 1979, I attended a meeting of people who were trying to re-establish a campaign for a Scottish Assembly. It was like a re-run of a bad B-movie. Everyone there wanted something different from the status quo but they were a hundred miles from any basic agreement on what the alternative should be. They wanted an Assembly but could not agree on its powers. At that meeting there seemed to be little understanding of how Scotland's condition under Mrs Thatcher's government would deteriorate fast and that the mild devolution measures proposed between 1974 and 1979 would not meet the need by the time we reached 1984. I left the meeting early but I had heard enough to convince me that, while an all-party effort was better than nothing, at the end of the day only decisive political action on a clear-cut constitutional position would break Scotland out of its English prison. I decided to think seriously about joining the SNP. It was the first time I had ever contemplated such an action.

It was by no means easy to think of such a step. I recognised that with the SLP gone there was no other instrument available to fight for the Scottish cause. But I remained a socialist, and so much of what the SNP leadership said was a denial of the validity of socialist reading of Scottish history and the need for socialist solutions to the problems created by our capitalist history. Those doubts about the SNP were based upon political principle.

There were other considerations. I had just spent over four years having my character attacked for leaving the Labour Party and had been widely accused of every political crime in the book. Turncoat, megalomaniac, traitor, fool, ratting on my friends, etc., etc. The smears at the personal level, especially around South Ayrshire, would have made *Private Eye* blush. To join a third party would only invite further abuse. To join the SNP was more than joining another party. The battles I had fought as a unionist against the SNP had left scars and bruises among people in their ranks, and whatever changes had arisen in my views on the Scottish question, I was still regarded with bitterness in certain quarters. I could not in all fairness expect those people to accept me as some sort of prodigal son. If I joined, I was bound to be attacked inside and pelted from outside. I decided to think it over.

The truth is that all of my actions in politics have been based upon a sense of responsibility and a belief that people in public life have a duty to act for the general good, even if that means risk at the personal level. I have always been prepared to risk my own earning capacity, my reputation and standing in pursuit of policies that would assist in the liberation of the Scottish working class. Such a fundamental attitude should be prudently tempered with caution so that if sacrifice is going to be made then it must be over something big. When I left the Labour Party, it was on a big issue and time has proved those of us who formed the SLP to have been right. There is no Scottish Assembly and the people are demoralised.

It has always been difficult for people to believe that I acted and continue to act from principle. Our politics are debased. People have become so used to politicians squirming and shifting, always self-seeking, never allowing themselves to be pinned down. This has meant that anyone who, particularly in Scotland, talks about making personal sacrifices is regarded as a bigger liar than the rest.

During the winter and spring of 1979-80, I faced yet another difficult choice. Unlike many others, I had never lost faith in the people. My continual analysis on what had gone wrong led me to see that they were victims and not culprits and I elaborate on this later in this book. Two things dominated my thinking. One that something had to be done to get things moving again. Two that no matter how disturbing, the fact was that only the SNP now represented a genuine alternative to the unionist parties.

Fortunately, there had been a significant development inside the SNP with the emergence of the '79 Group, whose commitment was to a socialist Scotland. The Group had experienced a rough passage at the first SNP conference after its formation but it was still there and growing. I went along as a guest speaker to a couple of its meetings and was impressed by their efforts to introduce the class factor into SNP politics. The existence of the Group was crucial for me. The SNP leadership might not like it but they had allowed the Group to settle and expand and so there was no longer a serious barrier to a socialist joining the party and doing so openly as a socialist.

I made up my mind to join in April 1980. But I waited for the local district council election results in May. If they were good for the SNP I would not join because I would be accused of jumping on a new bandwaggon. If they were bad, then I would join as no one could take much exception to a rat jumping *onto* a sinking ship. In the event the results were bad. So, in May 1980 I became a member of the SNP and within a few weeks the bitterness I anticipated came out in full flood. Some people were kind and happy to see me in. Others were deeply resentful and suspicious. That contradictory reaction created tensions which in turn were a great burden and proved damaging to some of the initiatives I was able to take as an office-bearer between 1981 and 1983.

However, there is a different story. Friends insist that I should go into revealing detail about my two years as Executive Vice-Chairman for Policy, particularly the events surrounding the internal sabotage of our civil disobedience campaign and the attempted expulsion of the '79 Group members. But I think it wise to resist. To pull open the door of the dirty linen cupboard would delight opponents of the SNP and would divert attention from the purpose of this book which is to explore issues of merit.

It is enough to note that despite its traumas, and perhaps because of them, the SNP has survived as a viable force. It is a much more mature organisation than that which was catapulted onto the scene in the late 1960s and early 1970s. Moreover, it has a growing number of young people who are breaking through into leadership positions. They must be encouraged to look back coolly and not in anger.

In this part of my contribution I have charted a long journey from a unionist background to the belief I had formed in 1979 about the necessity for Scottish independence. It does not cover the years from 1980 to the present because I have not been at the centre of political activity in Scotland. In the years since my defeat in South Ayrshire, I have travelled and worked in many parts of the Third World and the Middle East and my range of contacts and experience has widened enormously. I understand far more about international politics, economics, the importance of culture and the emotions that sway humankind than I ever knew when serving as a Member of Parliament. It has been an enriching experience and my gratitude for that extends to many people of many nationalities, especially a Kuwaiti friend who has taught me much but who loves anonymity and would not welcome even a grateful personal mention.

Placed on the fringes of Scottish politics and sometimes going out of the country for long periods, I have been able to think and analyse. During the contemplation of this book, the old working-class inhibitions surfaced again. Was I really able enough to write a book? Would my scant knowledge of grammar, my split infinitives not open me to ridicule? The inhibitions disappeared because "frankly" (to use Teddy Taylor's favourite word) I don't care what critics may say. Experience shows that unless people from Scotland's working class are prepared to articulate their thoughts, as best they can, no one will do it for them with accuracy.

I don't claim to speak for the Scottish working class. I speak for myself as one of them. The other part of this book contains essays. In my last few years of thinking and wondering, I have formed views on a number of issues thought to be important in the political development of the self-government movement. I trust that my thoughts will be of some service to the Scottish community.

*Part 2:*

## SCOTTISH THEMES

*Chapter 4*

# THE SCOTTISH LEFT AND THE NATIONAL QUESTION

"The cause of world socialism for which he lived has not yet been won but I am quite confident that the Scottish working class will play an honourable and noteworthy part in its achievement."

—Nan Milton on John MacLean

HOW SOCIALISTS RESOLVE the conflict between the needs of nationalities to express their collective will through self-determination and the concept of internationalism as a force demolishing barriers that divide the peoples of the world is extremely important.

The National Question, as the issue is known, has never produced a satisfactory answer around which all socialists could settle in theoretical comfort. It is a matter that has troubled greater minds and deeper intellects than mine. For a time, in the early development of socialist thinking, it was believed that international working-class solidarity, forged in a common struggle against capitalism, would be immune to the drumbeat of "national interests" and the call of patriotism. That belief was demolished by the carnage of the 1914-18 war, when workers from the most advanced capitalist countries engaged in mutual slaughter. Since then socialist thinkers have approached the issue of nationalism with caution, anxiety and uncertainty.

Nationalism is a phenomenon with which socialist theory is uncomfortable. It is a product which history, culture and social

83

development, as well as economic forces, have helped shape. However correct today's modern thinkers might be about the obsolescence of the nineteenth-century nation-state, the sense of nationhood among peoples remains a virile and potent force. Like it or lump it, the National Question remains an unanswered challenge. Tom Nairn brings this out well in his contribution to *The Red Paper on Scotland*, published in 1975:

> Intellectuals on the Left have spent much time trying to categorise forms of nationalism into the clean and the dirty, the "progressive" and the "reactionary" (or imperialist) and so on. And it is of course true that nationalisms differ according to where their nations stand in the general development process, those on top being more likely to be oppressive and unliberating in content. However, this sort of classification often conceals the fact *all* national ideologies are in reality "clean" *and* "dirty", containing progressive and highly regressive elements.

When confronted with nationalism the socialist thinker becomes confused. There is a certain underlying arrogance in the intellectual make-up of socialism in that there is a belief that the "correct" analytical approach can produce understanding, and a solution to a problem. The idea that there are human activities and attitudes that will confound the analyst is a little foreign to many in the movement. It comes as a shock, therefore, when a force such as nationalism presents itself in various forms and cannot be made to conform to conclusions based upon theoretical models.

Many outside the socialist movement must wonder at why the National Question should loom so large in our consideration of human development. Socialism needs a sound theoretical basis for its actions and policies because it is not simply concerned with putting this or that right in the economic life of a society. Its purpose is to change the nature of humankind, to civilise by promoting the needs of the whole community above the venal interests spawned by a profit-motivated capitalist society. Socialists need a framework of reference, fundamental points of principle and socialist verities on which they can build the new world. In many ways socialism is a religion which relies upon eternal truths to keep the faithful free from traps and temptations as the world spins and its human population behaves in ways unthought of and not anticipated by the founding fathers. If socialists are going to build a new world, they need to know why and on what foundation they will build, and the principles of construction.

One of the main principles of socialism is internationalism. A means whereby workers of the world will unite to form a brotherhood of man. Racism, hatred, bigotry, age-old antagonisms and poisoned fruits of past ages when the poor were universally exploited and manipulated by governing classes are to be eliminated by a new order. This new order will see people become masters and not victims of economic forces and the need to fight or compete with each other is replaced by co-operative action. It is of fundamental importance, therefore, to address as a matter of principle the apparent contradiction between nationalism and internationalism and reach an answer.

In passing, it must be said that the Labour movement in the United Kingdom has had a traditional aversion to matters theoretical. The failure to address the National Question and settle upon a principled position is a handicap to the Scottish Left in particular and has immobilised it at precisely the time when it needs to act decisively.

To explore the possible unity or discord between internationalism and nationalism, it is important to start with definitions which are so often missing in the verbal battles between the nationalist and the anti-nationalist Left in Scotland. Let us start with internationalism. Earlier I described the idea of creating a new world order in fairly utopian terms. That was not unfair because that is how the rhetoric often presents it. Indeed, the vision of a world where harmony and co-operation replaces killing and cut-throat marketplace competition is a powerful ideal with great attraction for the socialist movement. It is not my intention to debunk it however far the vision fails to correspond with reality. I can no more abandon the ideal of internationalism than can a Christian give up God because there is so much evil and horror to be found in His creation.

Old-time socialists used to equate internationalism with the concept of world government. But times have changed. We now live in a world of four billion people, gathered in different political systems and, quite properly, holding fast to a variety of cultures. Countries and states are all at different levels of development. Most important of all, we have a world power system which, like development, is unevenly distributed. There are super-powers but no single power or bloc can impose a single view on the whole human world.

In this complex and paradoxical world, it is difficult to fashion even a theoretical model of an administrative framework for world government and impossible to conceive of a universal political system that would be acceptable to even a small proportion of the world's people and their leaders. This means that the idea of internationalism must operate at a less utopian level. It must not offer one attainable goal but advance by a series of limited concrete objectives to which people can, from time to time, surrender what is their own vested interest for the greater good of the whole world.

The fact that in our present state of development humanity cannot go beyond ad hoc measures of international co-operation should not blunt our optimism or squeeze our spirit. Each time we carve out an area of agreement and sink part of our own sovereignty in the common world pool of decision-making, humanity takes a stride nearer salvation. H. G. Wells, writing in support of this ad hoc approach, put it much more eloquently than I can:

> The world may discover that all its common interests are being managed as one concern, while it still fails to realise that a world government exists. But before even so much human unity is attained, before such international arrangements can be put above patriotic suspicions and jealousies, it is necessary that the common mind of the race should be possessed of that idea of

human unity and the idea of mankind as one family should be a matter of universal instruction and understanding.

H. G. Wells: *A Short History of the World*

The practical task for socialists is to foster that idea of humankind as one family, living on one finite earth in which all must balance rights with responsibilities and obligations. This can best be done by engaging in the practical world of international relations, making an effort to consolidate and improve international bodies. Circumstances force upon us a step-by-step approach through the maze of bodies and agencies by which the world community seeks to regulate its relations. It is no simple task and presents great challenges, not least to patience and the purity of one's intentions.

It is particularly in the field of trade that socialists face the sternest test of internationalism. Whether it be in textiles, steel-making, engineering, motor vehicles or other manufactures, without overall world economic growth, an increase in Third World production and access to markets means job losses in the developed countries. Striking a balance between the needs of the Third World and the limits of workers' tolerance in the developed world is a delicate judgement and one that cannot be avoided. But of course we are not always faced with tension and potential conflict between the forces of the Third World and the economic interests of labour in the developed world. In an age of transnational companies, there is an urgent need to develop worker solidarity across geographic and national boundaries, creating a united front. While in the political field the Western socialist must be totally committed to the Third World's political struggle for freedom and the right of people within the Third World to rid themselves of despots and corruption.

By the very nature of our lives, it is easy to become absorbed in the problems presented by one's own society. Occasionally we are shocked into an international perspective by the tragedy of famine in Africa but the vast amount of our energies and interests are directed towards our own existence. Yet, if we are to promote the idea of human unity, of the race as one family, we must make a conscious effort to set out areas for international attention and action, which command the participation of the socialist movement. For that we need a motive. For socialists the motive is our "internationalism". But, what exactly is meant by that?

Internationalism is a state of mind, a set of attitudes which helps one human being empathise with others of different cultures, histories and social systems. A state of mind which recognises that there is no single national point of truth and certitude in any issue but that all people have rights and that mutual comprehension of that superior truth should lead to the resolution of conflicting interests through negotiation and give and take. It is a state of mind that admits that whatever proprietorial rights one's own national grouping may have on part of this earth and surrounding waters, they cannot be used selfishly and without regard to the welfare of people in other countries. It is a state of mind that has profound respect for the different cultures that world humanity has created and that rejoices in this rich variety of human endeavour. It is a set of attitudes that promotes a desire to see humankind blessed by universal principles of ethical conduct and which feels the pain when the human dignity of others is violated. The fact that internationalism is more a state of mind than a set of unchanging, concrete policies does not relegate its importance. Indeed, the concept is enhanced by having its source in our mental being. What raises humanity above other species is our mind and all our actions flow from whatever state it is in.

How can one fit Scottish nationalism into that basic intellectual concept and the framework of a practical internationalism? How can the Scottish people, as a separate entity, give more of their concern, active participation, positive political and logistical support and financial resources to progressive internationalism than they can do as part of the British State? We can do this by considering "nationalism". I see a nation as formed by people with a shared historical experience whose customs, practices, social mores, culture, patterns of thought and attitudes form a human group which is quite a distinct part of humanity. When that nation can identify issues and perceive that its members have a broad common interest in them and when that nation asserts its right to decide its own attitudes to issues then we have a basic nationalism. Usually a group's perception of its own nationhood is accompanied by an implicit or explicit demand that the rest of the world recognise its separate identity. It does not follow that all groups who can perceive of a common "national" identity and interest want or need to turn their nationhood into statehood. There are many multinational states. The United States, the USSR, India, New Zealand, Belgium, Yugoslavia, Czechoslovakia and Malaysia are but a representative sample. But there are others who take a different view, equating their distinctive nationhood with statehood. The Moslems of Mindanao in the Phillippines, the Basques, the Khurds, Israelis, the Poles, Egyptians, Persians, French, Swedes, Cubans and the English are examples.

Here the sceptic will interpose the view that this is all very well but that nationalism when it combines with statehood must of necessity narrow a people's perspective and, moreover, history shows that nationalism makes a people easy prey to evil. We are back to the intellectual fankle mentioned by Tom Nairn. History does indeed prove this, when nationalism is based upon assertions of inherent racial or cultural superiority, the people turn in upon themselves and develop a diabolical insensitivity to other nations. That kind of nationalism can lead people to evil and that cannot be denied. On the other hand there is evidence that when a nation does no more than assert the economic, social and cultural integrity of a distinctive group of people, insists that while they are no better than anyone else, they are no worse; insists upon a full entitlement to exercise freedom of judgement in both internal and external policies and contributes constructively to the world's life, it presents dangers to none. This is the twentieth-century position of Scandinavian nationalism. So, Tom Nairn's point about the categorisation

D

of nationalism into the "dirty" and "clean" seems proved. No doubt if one burrowed through the Swedish, Norwegian, Finnish and Danish brands of nationalism one would find regressive as well as progressive impulses. The socialist purist might then claim to rest his case because the admission that however nice and mundane are the Scandinavians, or the Fijians, evil having been done in the name of nationalism elsewhere puts it beyond the pale of acceptance: that would not be a balanced view.

Nationalism can be employed to drive people to stupidity, wrong and evil deeds. It can also inspire people to defend and advance basic human rights and dignities. In fact, nationalism is no different from any of the other "isms" which gain the loyalty of millions. There are a number of these great body of beliefs to which people surrender their critical faculties and often their souls. All of these "isms" seem able to captivate the minds of men and women and all have a bloody history, some of very recent date. None would pass the test of being judged by all the fruit it has borne.

Take socialism. Stalin and his followers enslaved and killed millions when, by terror, he pursued a version of socialism inherited from Lenin and Marx. A version, as Robert Conquest points out in his book on Lenin, that was flawed by the absence of a theory of political liberty. A rigorous examination of all that took place inside the USSR does not allow us to pin all the blame on Stalin as if he was an aberration. For all his genius, Marx had no working theory for a socialist state. Robert Conquest quotes Bukanin putting his finger on this "great flaw in the Marxist state":

> Those previous workers having just become rulers or representatives of the people will cease being workers; they will look at the workers from their heights, they will represent not the people but themselves. . . . He who doubts it does not know human nature.
> Robert Conquest: *Lenin*

Atrocity in the name of socialism did not begin and end with

Stalin. The cultural revolution in China and Pol Pot in Kampuchea are recent rotten fruits on the socialist tree.

The same strictures can be made about the other "isms". The advance and defence of capitalism, "dripping with blood from head to foot" as John MacLean said at his trial, has created oceans of grief. Christianity produced the Inquisition and has seen Protestant and Catholic butcher each other without pity, even up to the present day. India was partitioned in a wave of religious savagery as Moslem and Hindu gave vent to deep-seated hatred and fear. Even within its own body, Islam has spilt the blood of Shi'ite and Sunni. All of the great "isms" have in their time remorselessly persecuted minorities and heretics. All "isms" have inflicted pain and injustice when taken to extremes. All are capable of being "clean" and "dirty", containing progressive and highly regressive elements. We don't damn socialism or any of the others as absolutely evil. We discriminate, accepting one form of activity and belief while rejecting other repugnant actions and attitudes arising from the same body of ideology or views. There is no honesty in extending this discrimination to socialism and Christianity, for example, and withholding it from nationalism.

What would the discriminating say about Scottish nationalism? There are those who will claim it as chauvinistic and anti-English. They will be able to pray in aid evidence from speeches and propaganda put out, chiefly, by the traditional wing of the SNP. In that traditionalist group there is more than a touch of xenophobia and anglophobia and it would be foolish and dishonest to deny it. It is not my intention to offer an apologia for the traditionalists' anglophobia but they cannot be fairly or fully understood, or put into perspective, without reference to that other more potent variety of British nationalism — English nationalism and its concomitant, anglicisation. The process of anglicisation in the British Isles has been so pervasive and successful that the different cultures, languages, social attitudes and even institutions of the non-English have been relegated, mostly, to second best. They are on the "Celtic fringe", a phrase born in England to indicate the minor importance of other nations. Of course, in Scotland we have our own distinctive educational, religious and legal institutions but the character and standing of these have been subject to steady erosion and encroachment by anglicised ideas and practice.

It has been an insidious spread of one culture, reflecting the sad reality that constitutional Unions, which supposedly created the United Kingdom, were triumphs for English policy. We are not a union of equal partners, merely the English state continuing with Scottish and Welsh appendages which, in the course of time, while retaining some of their special character, will be more or less regions and not nations.

The strongly anti-English reaction of the traditionalist is based upon an acute awareness of how anglicisation diminishes the Scots. This understanding has been compounded by frustration and despair as Scotland has slipped from national towards provincial status, with hardly a whimper from her people. Traditionalists have been forced to spend their lives defensively poking fingers in the Scottish dam as it crumbles under the weight of English culture and general policy. This defensive, soul-destroying rôle has produced nationalists weighed down with grievance, whose emotions are wracked by every little symbol of English hegemony. It has produced people with raw touchy emotions and reactions which can appear to their fellow citizens as sometimes ridiculous and sometimes ugly. They are, in Tom Nairn's words, the regressive element in Scottish nationalism. Fortunately, they do not represent the whole of Scottish nationalism. There is another progressive element, first formalised by the '79 Group and still developing, whose members have avoided the swampland of grudge. They are as much aware of anglicisation as any traditionalist but realise that in an unequal union where there has been a dramatic difference in population and power between Scotland and England, the larger would always naturally threaten to overwhelm the smaller.

There is in this school the understanding that there has been no English malice in the process, just the unconscious thrusting upon others of the culture, outlook and policy of the numerically stronger nation for whose principal benefit the whole constitutional set-up was engineered. It is of course not something that is acceptable and progressive nationalists are as determined as any traditionalist to remove Scotland from this overwhelming English influence, which has been responsible for so much malformation in our nation's intellectual, cultural and social development.

In the last few paragraphs I have tended to dwell upon the forms of nationalism within the ranks of the SNP. But we have to judge on a wider scale, despite the public declarations and postures of the SNP being frequently taken as a guide to the real state of nationalism. How the Scots in general form and articulate their nationalism is *the* critical factor. It has to be said that they have proved remarkably immune to the promptings of the traditionalists and many an SNP canvasser can testify to the distaste with which the average elector responds to strident anti-Englishism.

The Scottish people's relationship with the English is a complex one. There is a lack of self-confidence in the face of implied English superiority and this sometimes manifests itself in absurd gestures of over-compensation especially in the world of football where the biennial Wembley game assumes an importance which it does not warrant. It is a personal opinion but I shall believe Scotland has sorted out its inferiority complex when Wembley becomes just another game, good to win but not a Flodden if lost. But there are other factors at work, historical, social and economic. In the growth and struggles of the trade union movement, the Scottish and English working classes have formed a common bond and, while differences of interest do arise from time to time, there is a common interest and outlook in matters affecting workers' rights and liberties. We also have to take into account the extensive social intercourse that the Union of 1707 has brought in its train and the effects of the free flow of people between the two countries. There can hardly be a family in Scotland without a relative in England and this fact alone militates against the Scots seeing the English as foreign devils.

Of no small significance are the commercial and industrial links forged by the respective business communities. By no means do these links eliminate feelings of national difference. In recent years Scottish business interests have become aware of just how much control has slipped from them to contemporaries in the south and there is resentment. But that resentment is tempered through the personal relations and contacts which arise when business is done on a continuing basis.

The outward-looking progressive nationalism to be found left of centre in the SNP mirrors the instinct and inclination of the Scottish people as a whole. This progressive nationalism is developing in response to economic and political trends in both Scotland and England. There has been an unmistakable drift to the right in English politics as English capitalism has shifted its base from north to south and as the post-Empire decline has produced a need for scapegoats because of an in-built resistance to facing fundamental problems with fundamental solutions. In the common market of Britain, where Scottish power is non-existent and our influence weak, and where England can no longer ameliorate the effects of industrial decline with regional policies, the Scottish economy has reached its own special crisis. More and more people are coming to realise that effective crisis management and effective policies for long-term recovery can only come from within Scotland and that no one is coming to our aid because they have no aid to give.

There are, therefore, natural political and economic forces at work, opening a gulf between the Scottish and English political systems. We are witness to a process of national self-determination on the part of both nations. The fulcrum of power in England has shifted southwards to the conservative areas and thus there has been an irreversible move to the right.

94

In moving to the right, England's people are exercising a shift in national policy in pursuit of their national interest. Scotland on the other hand, where the small population creates a greater homogeneity, has not followed the English conservative drift. Scots are coming to perceive their national interests as different and better served by a different political philosophy and economic programme. In this circumstance, progressive Scottish nationalism and its growing demand for self-government is a legitimate refusal to have Scottish democratic opinion swamped by contrary English democratic opinion. Just as there was no malice in England's exercise of hegemony, there is none in progressive nationalism's drive to escape permanent subjugation to that hegemony when to do so means accepting the unacceptable. It is a natural drawing apart of two systems and societies with less and less in common, and fewer mutual interests.

What is emerging is an active and progressive nationalism, not ugly, not born of a desire to do down anyone else, with a wish to free the energies and attributes of the Scottish people so that they can engage not only on the reconstruction of our own society but on the problems that keep the vast mass of humanity in a miserable existence.

This brings us back to the question put earlier. Can the objective of Scottish nationalism, that is the creation of a Scottish state, succeed in giving more to international causes than the Scots can accomplish as part of the British state? First, we need to realise that the internationalist Scot is going to accomplish less and less for the poor of the world and for strengthening international co-operation within the present British state. That state is in perpetual crisis arising out of remorseless decline and its Establishment will cut the aid programme time and again in future years. The same Establishment will continue to side with the reactionary forces in the world. *A right-wing British state is a prison for the Scottish progressive spirit.* Second, an independent Scotland, even one with a policy of oilsharing, would have resources well beyond her own needs. These resources mean that although we are a small country, as a major oil producer well into the twenty-first century, we would have political and economic influence quite disproportionate to our size. This latter point is not one I want to exaggerate. However, an independent oil-exporting Scotland as a full voting member of the EEC (as I argue elsewhere) would carry its own weight and sometimes the borrowed weight of the whole Community. That weight, of a radical committed Scotland, would be thrown in favour of the world's disadvantaged.

A progressive Scotland as a member of the IMF, the World Bank, GATT, UNCTAD and the United Nations, would not rank as a major power. But like Norway and Sweden, small, prosperous, but concerned and active on the international scene, there would be yet another European voice raised on the side of the Third World, pushing especially for greater Third World participation in the policy-making of the IMF and World Bank.

Last, but not least, and this can only happen if Scotland is independent, we could pursue an ambitious aid policy. As Kuwait and other Arab countries have done, we could set up a special development fund to provide technical and financial assistance to the poorest and most vulnerable developing countries. Whatever are our instincts and impulses now, Scottish socialists and others of a radical bent are spectators in the international struggle for freedom and justice. We cannot give direct substantial aid to Nicaragua, mobilise resources to help combat South Africa's destabilisation of front-line African states, nor stretch our hand of help to Tanzania in its effort to remain free from the grip of the IMF. Nor as things stand now, with Scotland a provincial backwater without power and influence, can we ensure that our contribution to, for example, UNICEF, comes anywhere near matching that organisation's needs in saving, as it could, the lives of ten million children a year. The following table of payments to UNICEF show just how impotent is a non-independent Scotland:

|                | *$ per head of population* |
|----------------|----------------------------|
| Norway         | 4.75                       |
| Sweden         | 3.75                       |
| Denmark        | 3.85                       |
| United Kingdom | 0.17                       |

That level of support, 17 cents, is fairly typical of the United Kingdom's approach to aid. While Labour governments have a better record than does the present Tory administration, the difference is marginal.

For years now I have heard speakers from the British Labour Party argue that their internationalism precludes any truck with Scottish nationalism. By internationalism they invariably but unconsciously mean British nationalism, frequently exhibited by a bit of French-bashing or threatening the EEC with British Gaullism. However, I shall not pursue the flagrant contradiction between their claim to internationalism and their parochial policies. What has to be challenged is their adherence to a political system (the constitutional union with England) that blocks the Scottish impulse to join directly in the effort to free the world's people from want and hunger.

Finally, there are the consequences for Scotland's working people if significant sections of the Left, the Labour Left, continue to follow an infantile version of internationalism. These so-called internationalists expatiate with fervour on setting the working people of the world free from the influences of international capitalism but it is not in their direct power to set free the people of any country, except one. They cannot, for example, exercise control over the fate of black South Africans or the Poles or the peoples of Central and South America. We can all help those people through moral, political and economic action but the doctrine of non-intervention, to which socialists attach so much importance, means that direct active involvement is ruled out. Therefore, no matter how sincere we are in seeking to help, there are physical and political limits placed upon us.

The one country the Labour Left can help liberate, by direct action and without diplomatic, political or trading inhibitions, is Scotland. It is acknowledged that Scotland has the greatest penetration by transnational companies in the whole of Western Europe, that we have massive poverty and criminal levels of unemployment in a land through which oil wealth passes at a rate of £1,000 million each month and that we are controlled by a government we did not elect. It is not so much an irony as a tragedy that the Labour Left will not free the only people they have it in their power to help directly.

Faced with the grave effects of the United Kingdom's industrial collapse and the rising demand in Scotland for some meaningful control of economic affairs through a directly elected Parliament, the Labour Left continue to hide behind a slogan of "internationalism". In their case it is a term without substance, merely a word to camouflage confusion and irresolution, at best a neat barrier to raise against disturbing analysis and thought. But we on the non-Labour Left shoulder part of the blame. We have let our friends get away with dodging the need to examine the issues of Scottish nationalism and genuine internationalism, we have been defensive and apologetic. We must now be assertive.

*Chapter 5*

# THE SCOTTISH PEOPLE:
# CULPRITS OR VICTIMS?

A FEW DAYS before polling in the devolution referendum of 1979, the *Glasgow Herald* cartoonist, Turnbull, drew his now famous Scottish Lion, lying down saying, when faced with the prospect of responsibility that goes with self-government, "I'm feart." That image was confirmed, so it seemed, by the narrow Yes majority of the final result and by the failure of the Scots to leap over the 40 per cent barrier, a blocking measure introduced by Labour MPs and supported by the Tories. It is an image that haunts all who favour self-government, of whatever degree. They are plagued by the question: are the Scottish people weak in character, a craven lot who will let themselves down again?

Many people who poured their whole lives into the fight for a Scottish Assembly have a deep anxiety that another similar effort will end in another fiasco. At various meetings, private and public, one hears statements such as, "the Scots have no guts", "the Scots are crippled by a lack of self-confidence", "they are getting what they deserve", or, to quote the then senior vice-chairman of the SNP writing in *The Scotsman* in 1984, "the stupidity of the Scottish people has cost them dear". Since the political collapse immediately following on the 1979 Referendum, we have experienced an industrial collapse. With a few exceptions, the workforce in establishment after establishment has lain down in the face of massive redundancies. This had led to a lack of confidence *in the people* among political and industrial leaders. The leader writers, politicians and senior trade unionists make no clarion calls for the nation to rise and demand justice. All are reduced to a plaintive wail about the lack of will and spirit. How justified is this lack of confidence in the people? Are the people culprits or are they victims? That is what I want to examine.

The Scots are a nation with a history about which a great number know nothing. A people who, with Gaelic in some areas and braid Scots in others, along with the employment of the English language, can reach great heights of eloquence and expression yet succumb easily to the myth of their own literary and intellectual inadequacies — a myth imposed by the unrelenting pressures of a neighbouring culture and the desertion of Scottish standards by the aristocracy and the middle classes who were masters of the Scottish political scene for the first decisive century of the Union. The fruits of the Union, the price of being the northern province of the English state, is a split personality and a nation uncertain about its own worth. In all the many countries I have visited, only in Scotland have I found people from all walks of life who will seriously put forward the proposition "we are not fit to run our own affairs".

One might have hoped that the modern political system produced by extensions of the franchise and the rise of the Labour movement would have helped mend the Scottish personality, but no. Scotland's modern politicians have been accommodated and woven into the English system and absorbed by its Parliament. They have their own Scottish Grand Committee, Scottish Standing Committees for examining legislation in detail. They get the occasional full day of debate on the Scottish economy on the floor of the House of Commons and there is a Select Committee on Scottish Affairs, through which eleven of our seventy-two MPs are supposed to investigate the government's handling of Scottish policy. This whole apparatus maintains a Scottish identity at a parochial level, while the big stuff like Defence, Foreign Policy, Industrial Relations, Energy, Trade, and Economic Policy is dealt with at the English/British level. Thus the "split" is reinforced.

Perhaps, given that England was a great power with an empire, it was inevitable that its system would seduce the Scottish political class soon after the Union articles were signed. After all, the Scots were given a share of that English power, conditional upon accepting its source. Scottish industrial and commercial interests were given unhindered access to the lucrative markets of the Empire. Those were the days before democracy and, anyway, the Scots' governing classes had never shown much basic patriotism.

The disenfranchised classes, who had been unhappy about the Union, continued to cling to their Scottish identity — and there were sporadic demands for Home Rule. But it was never independence, except in the Insurrection of 1820 when the slogan was "Scotland Free or a Desert". Prophetic. The norm has been demands for Home Rule within the Empire or Commonwealth. There have been many Home Rule Bills presented in the House of Commons seeking some sort of Scottish self-government. There has never been a single English Home Rule Bill: such is not necessary because England never lost its independence in 1707.

The Second World War, when so many previous conventional beliefs and norms were swept aside for ever in that cathartic experience, should have given the Scots an opportunity to struggle clear of their "British or Scottish?" dilemma, or at least firmly resolve the problem of what is the prime identity. But post-1945 Britain saw an unprecedented process of centralisation as the new Labour government tackled reconstruction and built the foundations of the welfare state. Scotland's political class was deeply affected by this phenomenon: they were cast not in the role of genuine leaders addressing how we rebuilt our part of Western Europe (even as part of a multinational state) using our own traditions and social values as well as our economic potential, but as lobbyists. Lobbyists whose "national" character gave them an edge on those bidding for central government attention from the likes of Merseyside and Durham.

A political class should provide a forum in which a nation examines, discusses and debates its internal affairs, its social and economic development, as well as the set of criteria, moral, cultural, aesthetic and material, by which we measure "development". It should also be concerned with our external relations. A political class should also look ahead, identifying both problems and opportunities. That is the leadership rôle. The Scottish political class has played no such rôle. The people have been left to hang as they grow.

There are, of course, reasons for the failure of our political class to give positive national leadership. The programmes for post-war reconstruction meant that the power to draw in and allocate resources at the centre of government in London had greatly increased. This lent a new dimension of decision-making in Whitehall-based ministries which already had long years of administrative responsibility. The science, or art, and practice of governing was enhanced by these developments. Although the Scottish Office did benefit from the tenure of Tom Johnston during the war years, no future Secretary of State was to possess his imagination or influence. Johnston commanded the post on his own merits and from a powerful political base. All who succeeded him were place-men, dependent upon and never in a position to dictate to the Prime Minister. The Scottish Office was 400 miles away from the new growth of central power with only a small skeleton staff in Whitehall. This meant that Scottish Ministers and MPs were not part of the Whitehall Mandarin circle and were thus excluded from the kind of day-to-day intimate contact between the great departments of state; they were at least one remove from the real decision-making process.

It has been a different matter with the English political class. They swarmed and continued to swarm around London where they provide a genuine national forum for England's debates about itself and its external relations. A political class is, of course, politicians, Ministers, shadow Ministers, policy-making senior civil servants, political scientists, prestigious institutes, head offices of pressure groups, senior staff and advisers of the party organisations, senior trade unionists, their industrial and business counterparts, the financial and banking powers and the media. But Parliament, the government, the TUC, the CBI, the City and all their trappings and hangers-on are the institutions of the English State, working in the capital of their country, serving their own and State interests. Whatever they may say in public about opposing each other (and much of it is true), they do value and gain from meeting formally within the vast machinery of government bodies and working parties and informally in the social gatherings, seminars and private meetings arranged by the various institutes and trusts. This has allowed the English political class to continue to function and continue its centuries-old practices of statecraft.

For the Scots, however, the position is very different. Government Ministers and MPs scatter to their constituencies when they return at weekends so the elected representatives, who create the magnetism in a democratic system, meet the rest of our political class all too infrequently and rarely in any informal way. Instead of developing and refining the habits and techniques required for *government* they, representing a province, have become expert at the lesser arts of lobbying the governors. For generations now, the Scots and their institutions have worn a groove on the road to London. "We" go down there and "They" give us something; thus Scotland's inferior status and begging-bowl mentality has emerged. Given the events surrounding the creation of the Union, the continuity for English political development and the discontinuity for the Scots, the end result was inevitable. It has also to be noted that while individual Scots have made it to the top of the English pole whether to Cabinet, senior places in the civil service, trade unions or industry, the Scottish political class as a whole has remained unco-ordinated and fragmented. Their collective views on any subject rarely disturb the waters in which the London establishment swim.

I have gone into a brief examination of what makes the Scottish and English system tick to demonstrate two things. First, that the people of Scotland have been subjected to strong unrelenting pressures on their culture and identity and their self-esteem for almost the whole period of the Union. A process that is demeaning and debilitating. Second, by the reduction of our political class to the rôle of pressure group (for that is what it is) we have never been able to acquire the diplomatic skills and power analysis needed to engage in the arts of statecraft in the affairs of the nation. The result is that Scotland is politically unsophisticated and has grown used to others, in England, taking the strain of the really big decisions.

Scots as a people have, in view of the pressures and circumstances, fallen prey to arguments that they are heavily subsidised by England and that if they took even half a step away from Big Brother it would mean ruin and disaster. In recent years facts have been produced purporting to clearly demonstrate this "beggar" and "giver" relationship. In 1968, under threat from a rising SNP tide, the Treasury published a Scottish budget, showing that a notional Scottish government would be in deficit. Since then tables are regularly published in the columns of *Hansard* showing that, per head of population, public spending is greater in Scotland than it is in England. Thus dependence and anxiety about the crumbs that now and then fall from the rich man's table has continued to shape the Scottish mentality.

At one time, with the rise of the SNP as a fresh element in Scotland's political class and the discovery of oil in Scottish waters of the North Sea, it looked as though Scotland would break free from its beggar mentality. The old arguments which had always succeeded in depressing any Scottish thoughts of independence — that we were too poor — were demolished by the revelation of the oil wealth that started to pour out in the 1970s. The Treasury produced no more Scottish budgets, even when repeatedly pressed to do so by the self-government movement. The potential embarrassment of each drop of the

104

magic oil was dealt with by the simple, crooked device of removing oil revenues from any purely Scottish statistics. It went instead into a special North Sea account. The fish caught and landed from Scottish waters are allowed to remain in Scotland's accounts but the oil over which those fish swim — well, that is different! But the Treasury need not have worried. Remember that the Scots have been saddled with two burdens. One, the belief that we are subsidised and poor and, the other, that we owe the English a great deal for past favours. While oil might have dispelled the first false belief, it did nothing for the latter feeling of indebtedness. In the event, it proved easy for the London establishment to neutralise the oil factor.

It is ironic that as oil production soared Scottish interest waned. By 1984, when North Sea production rates were the major influence in the world oil markets, it was impossible to get a flicker of interest on oil in the mind of the general public in Scotland. Not only were we the only nation ever to discover oil and get poorer, we were the only nation to strike a bonanza and believe it didn't matter. Oil was removed from the political equation by first deriding its importance and then, when the sheer volume of potential could not be denied, by mining that rich and deep seam of Calvinist guilt that is our collective inheritance from the Reformation. In the early days (and I confess my own sinful part in the tactics), the Labour Party put out leaflets entitled "Scotland Beware! . . . of dangerous myths", about the value of oil. Later, the tune changed and we in the Labour movement said bluntly that it was sheer greed to want the oil and that the nation should reject the siren voices which claimed that oil equalled prosperity. One prominent Labour activist went as far as to say on television that it could not be Scotland's oil because we didn't put it there: the clear implication being that we had no right to purloin or enjoy an accident of nature.

The Scots crumbled. The SNP case for using oil as a great capital asset, to rebuild the Scottish industrial capability, establish a superb economic and social infrastructure and place increased investment in our universities, colleges and schools fell upon increasingly deaf ears. The other part of the SNP case put, if I may say so, most cogently by Margo MacDonald, was never understood: the oil revenues, large as they were, could never transform the entire British economy because its problems were so deep seated and profound but the same oil, applied to the small size of the Scottish economy, would create a new era of dynamic growth.

Since the first oil began to flow, over £40 billion has poured into the UK Treasury. Little has dropped on the Scottish economy. Yet our southern partner's position has not been transformed: the decline in their economic performance has accelerated. Time has proved Margo correct.

It really does take a massive guilt complex and a belief in an enormous national debt to the English for the Scottish people to raise not a whimper at such a brazen theft. But what can one really expect of a people whose pressure group political class is too divided and weak to give real leadership? With the exception of the SNP, the political parties have dual loyalties, with London exerting a greater pull than Scotland. Our media is almost wholly controlled and owned by non-Scottish interests and seems incapable of sustaining any serious challenge to English policy. Our academic institutions have been pathetic, always trembling and anxious about how they will be dealt with by their paymasters of the southern dominated Universities Grants Committee. It is worth noting that the Labour Party, which in 1985 controls three Scottish regional councils and twenty-five Scottish district councils, covering about two-thirds of the entire country, all of them fighting for their financial lives against the Tory government, is keeping quiet on oil. There are no questions from them as to why, with the wealth pouring out, their authorities face cuts in essential services. When politicians in the Home Rule movement and the odd leader writer bemoan the lack of fight and self-confidence among the people, there should be a little more understanding about the events and circumstances which, on occasion, turn our people into putty.

With a conspiracy of silence between the Labour, Tory and Alliance parties on the oil issue, you cannot blame the people for their ignorance on the subject.

We also have to take into account why the window of opportunity, opened by the emergence of the SNP and their parliamentary gains in 1974, closed to such little effect by 1979. Did the fault lie with the people? Were they culprits or victims? Here, again, I believe a balanced look at events will acquit the people and indict the leadership. Here I refer, of course, to the new leadership that emerged in Scotland during the 1970s and to the people who took charge of the Home Rule movement's most successful political campaign to date. In my view, the Home Rule section of Scotland's political class did not perform well in handling the task of bringing something concrete out of the effort expanded in the years from 1974 to 1979. The reasons for that failure are what I want to explore but, in passing, I would ask the reader to note that the failure of the Home Rule leadership reinforced the people's fear about their own inadequacy. A people, whose cultural integrity and self-confidence has been underminded for two and a half centuries, needed a leadership which could out-debate, out-think, out-manoeuvre and be strategically superior to the London establishment. The Home Rule leadership never met that need.

The eleven SNP Members of Parliament elected in October 1974 and their senior officials and National Executive in Scotland, stand out as the main element in the Home Rule leadership. There were others, of whom the following are but a sample — John Mackintosh, John Robertson, Neal Ascherson, Bob Tait, Isobel Murray, Bob Brown, Joe Farrell, Alex Neil and myself. There were also the Liberals. We must never forget the Liberal leadership and the rôle it played. It is to all of these, including myself, that I direct criticism. It is not aimed destructively but is an objective assessment of how we let the people down. It is difficult for those who gave their all to a cause to accept that perhaps they failed to give of their best, or that their best was not good enough. Let me say immediately that all had fine motives. That is not in question. But we owe it to ourselves and the people to submit our performance to a searching enquiry; we should be unafraid to place blame on our own shoulders if that is necessary. We must not take the easy way out and blame the people. If we try to avoid our own inadequate rôle, then we only ensure that no lessons are learned and that old errors will be repeated.

The 1974-79 period was the first time ever that the Home Rule movement got into the big-time political league. There had been notable Home Rulers before, such as the Rev. James Barr and Jimmie Maxton, but they were cast within a larger grouping and frequently taken up with other issues. But here, in the 1970s, was a central core: the SNP, the Scottish Liberals, the SLP and the independent-minded, highly influential John Mackintosh. All were backed by a powerful nationalist current within the trade union movement and an intelligentsia thrusting forward with new ideas and confidence. All these and the Scottish constitutional position dominated centre stage in the British Isles. A review of the speeches made at that time shows that we all thought the tide would roll and roll and nothing could stop it. We failed completely to take account of the nature of the opposition — the two great parties of the English state, Labour and Tory, the power of the Whitehall departments and the deep reservoirs of experience these institutions had accumulated over many years in dealing with awkward problems that came from unexpected angles. The struggle of the New Commonwealth countries to overcome ploy after ploy to inhibit their advancement to independence and the Irish episode of British history were warnings of a considerable ability to stall new forces that threatened London's grip. With oil from Scotland, a God-sent gift to an ailing establishment, we should have known that they would play rough and crooked.

But none of us had any experience of carrying a major policy change against the wishes and will of a hostile governing force. Even John Mackintosh, author of a major work on the Constitution and a practising professor of Politics, had no actual experience of *realpolitik*. We all knew there was a fear of the forces let loose in Scotland. We thought the threats to Labour's political anchor and the implied threat to the future of oil revenues, if Parliament failing on devolution drove the Scots to independence, would be enough to gain a graceful, if reluctant, concession on self-government. We were blind to the fact that we were allowing every initiative to lie with our opposition. Let me be perfectly clear. By opposition I mean the Labour Cabinet, a majority of its backbenchers, the Tory Party, and the Whitehall machine. Although a Labour government produced the Scotland Bill and there were those such as Michael Foot who wanted to see it through, the fact remains that at no time would the Cabinet lay on a three-line whip when such action, taken as a vote of confidence, would guarantee passage of the Bill.

We believed that the vote gained by the SNP in 1974 and its string of spectacular bye-election wins in local government thereafter, meant that we had the initiative. But the reality was that government set the timetable, wrote the White Paper, drafted the Bill, determined how it would be handled in the House of Commons and who, if anyone, would get concessions by amendments or by private understandings. It was the official Tory Opposition who were entitled to the giant share of amendments. It was chiefly the Tories who cast the lures, by way of amendments, which allowed Labour backbenchers to revolt at will against their own government. The Labour Cabinet decided that there would be no disciplinary measures, no harsh words. The government held its hands to heaven proclaiming its hurt and innocence, while Cabinet Ministers were seen in private to smile encouragement at the rebels.

In other words, the Establishment was in the driving seat and yet we naïvely overlooked this great strategic and tactical advantage and thought that as long as we hung on, it was in the bag. In one speech in the House of Commons, I struck upon the nub of the matter when asking how does a Parliament pass a measure which it detests? Foolishly, as the wave of Scottish feeling swept on, I sought no answer. I would have served my country better by taking that question to pieces time and time again until the answer emerged: even if it does pass it, there will be a way found to prevent its implementation.

But I didn't probe. Nor did anyone else. At a time when we should all have been engaged in acute thinking and analysis, we enjoyed the emotional ride instead. At home the Assembly was taken for granted and a host of intelligent and committed people in all walks of life began to build up the new policies we would all bring forward for debate in our new Scotland. Had we all been prudent, the Establishment would not have been successful in pushing us in their desired direction, making us subject to the main thrust of their policy which was to wear down by attrition and win by chicanery.

Let us go through the mistakes of the Home Rule leadership. For me, thinking through to an admission of guilt, albeit shared, has been a chastening experience. However, I do not see an analysis and the conclusion that we made grave errors as totally condemnatory. Nor do I see past errors as justification for making no efforts in the future to advance the cause of self-government. As was pointed out earlier, 1974-79 was our first venture into the big league and, in hindsight, one can see that mistakes were inevitable. There is no cause for shame in that. It should be marked down to experience and make us more able to achieve success when we are coming within touching distance of our objective next time. But to the mistakes. First, we let the government set the timetable. They spun it out as long as they could before producing the key White Paper, buying almost six months of time by announcing a delay in the introduction of the legislation. I was then a member of the Labour Party and for internal reasons thought it wise to play down the significance of Harold Wilson's prevarication. In a speech made to a T&GWU meeting in Glasgow, on 21 November 1975, I said:

> In the last forty-eight hours reactions on the devolution question from certain quarters in Scotland have been hysterical and as foolish as the English backlash we have witnessed over recent weeks. Scottish paranoia is no more edifying than the English version.

110

> There is no doubt that any delay in the legislative process is a big disappointment but it need not, and must not, delay the date of the Assembly elections and the day when Scotland has its own Assembly meeting for the first time. Those are the two crucial dates, and as long as the legislative timetable meets them, there is no cause for deep cries of agony.

I recall telling a reporter that I was not too upset by the delay because "six months was not significant in the life of a nation". Little did I realise that six months' delay in the short life of a Parliament can be decisive. The SNP Group made a fuss but their sound seemed calculated to gain maximum party advantage and was far from a warning cry about an ultimate failure to deliver the Assembly. John Mackintosh though it was just a hiccup and the Liberals were sanguine. For all of us, the delay was less important than the contents of the much awaited White Paper setting out the Assembly powers. That constituted our next mistake. Although all parties and some individuals had written to the government about what we wanted to see in the White Paper, by and large the Home Rule leadership took a "wait and see" position. None of us put down markers to be built up in the public mind. We unknowingly were taking up a reactive rôle.

When the White Paper was published there was almost universal condemnation on grounds that the powers offered were inadequate. But this was a general reaction and not really very detailed. For instance, although that publication caused me to leave the Labour Party and the SNP and some newspapers to have a field day at the government's expense, we still put down no detailed markers about what should be in the Bill. Again, we waited to see what would happen. Always the government's proposals were measured against our general attitude defined loosely as "substantial powers", "real teeth", "financial powers" and other such imprecise formulations. The government's proposals were never once measured against a well-constructed alternative bill. We said roughly what we wanted but left it to them to say whether, or how, the objective would be met.

111

Ultimately, the Bill was tabled and debated and the voting started. From the outset, the hostility towards Scottish self-government was so intense that you could feel it. A coalition of Tory Party frontbench and Labour backbenchers began a successful filibuster. The government was forced into using the guillotine procedure to speed the Bill's passage. It was a trap set to defeat the Bill and it worked. After the government failed to carry the guillotine motion because Labour backbenchers rebelled and either voted with the Tories or abstained, we Home Rulers made another mistake, one that was to prove fatal. The morning after, it was apparent that the first Bill was dead, yet Labour's need to keep the Scottish issue on the agenda, for its own survival, remained paramount. Michael Foot quickly let it be known that there would be a second Bill: that was the Home Rule leadership's opportunity to go with a deal, seeking certain guaranteed powers for the Assembly in return for supporting the, by now, minority Labour government.

Here, the SNP proved the main stumbling block. Forgetting that a bird in the hand is worth two in the bush, they calculated that Labour's failure on the guillotine merely strengthened their position at home. The theory of the "rising tide of nationalism" washed away any doubts about the future. There was no real need to secure something in the present. As a party whose rôle was to seek independence, the SNP were anxious not to compromise their purity. But that meant rigidity when Scotland's interest called for flexibility and skilful manoeuvre. The other mistake at this juncture was to underestimate the English and the lengths they would go to cross party lines to cripple the Scottish effort towards self-government. We should have been warned and again we should have put down markers. We ignored all the danger signals. We produced no detailed structure of the kind of second Bill required. Again, we took up a reactive rôle.

Then came the two tactical strikes by Labour's anti-devolutionists and I have no doubt they were working in concert with the Tories. First, they demanded a referendum as a precondition to giving the government's second Bill a majority at Second Reading. We shrugged our shoulders and made jokes about the "Hefferendum" which upset Norman Buchan because he claimed the idea was his and not that of Eric Heffer, the Labour MP for Liverpool Walton. But getting agreement to include the Referendum as part of the Bill was only half the tactic. The other half came in setting down amendments to bring in the 40 per cent rule. This stated, it will be recalled, that unless 40 per cent of all those on the electoral register voted "Yes", the government would be bound in law to table a simple order to repeal the whole Scotland Act in one short day. This meant that those who traditionally take no part in the political process, those away from home and unable to get a postal vote, the dead and the names on the register in error would all count for the "No" side. The Home Rule leadership had acquiesced in the inclusion of the Referendum as part of the Scotland Bill but was now scandalised by the 40 per cent trick. But we actually did nothing. We failed to demonstrate in the House of Commons, get ourselves evicted and thus start to stir up concern among people back home.

Partly contributing to this whole shrug of the shoulders attitude remained the belief that even with a referendum, even with a 40 per cent rule, the Scots could carry anything before them in reaching for an Assembly. We were smitten with a romantic view of our people. Convinced that they would respond to the insult, we felt sure they would sweep over any blocking barrier. That optimistic view, founded on nothing but blind faith, also meant that we let through, with minimal fight, a set of referendum rules which were a disgrace to democracy. Those rules, which allowed the "No" side to spend at will, proved a serious handicap when the referendum campaign opened.

Let me just explain briefly why the referendum rules, or lack of them, were so important. In the 1975 EEC Referendum, it was recognised that there was a financial disparity between the "Yes" for staying in and "No" for coming out. The former were able to command greater resources. Parliament tried to right the balance by allowing each side a free leaflet and free postage to every home in the United Kingdom. The government, too, sent out a major statement to every home through the post. In addition, there was the equivalent of party political broadcasts by the opposing sides. There was also a grant of public money to both campaigns to ensure that a reasonable effort to reach the public would succeed. In the Scottish Referendum, there were no free leaflets and postage. The government did not send out a policy statement to any home. There were no party political style broadcasts. There were no cash grants to allow the financially weaker side to get its case across. The result was that the "Yes" side faced a "No" campaign backed by the Tory Party's full United Kingdom financial resources and direct help from big business. These were crippling factors.

That catalogue of mistakes was compounded by the divisions which prevented any united stance behind a "Yes" campaign when the Referendum got under way. I have dealt with this in the earlier part of the book but it is worth noting in passing that while Scotland's politicians were able to gather together in pursuit of their respective views on the EEC Referendum, they conspicuously failed to do so over the Scottish Assembly Referendum. All in all, it was a poor performance by the Home Rule leadership. Such an admission is not a cause for shame. Regret yes, but not shame. It is certainly no reason for damning the activists concerned from here to eternity. The Scottish political class lacked experience of statecraft and the Home Rule leadership was tossed a responsibility for which it was neither trained nor ready.

Like many others who exhausted energy and tossed aside a career in pursuit of some tangible self-government, my early reaction to the shambles was to look askance at the people. That view was founded in disappointment and despair. Shortly after the General Election of 1979, I began to think things through and submit those crucial years to a keener analysis. A walk in the wilderness can bring beneficial clarity to thought. It was we who

114

failed the people, not they who failed us. We, the Home Rule leadership and the Labour Party, were the real culprits. We meant well: the Labour Party played a double game and played it dirty. Given all the debilitating formative influences that bear upon the Scottish people, dragging them down into a self-deprecating rôle, they needed a brilliant leadership. One that would lift them onto a new plane of self-esteem and confidence and give them the gift of clarity of vision and thought. A leadership which, by its performance, would inspire confidence and impart strength. For all our qualities and sincerity, we did not provide that kind of leadership. The people were and are victims of our failure.

*Chapter 6*

# SCOTLAND'S PROBLEM: TITANIC ENGLAND

WHEN I WAS young and a member of the Labour Party, Scots lobbyists measured success by the number of industrial projects and regional grants they could extract from government in London. That led me and most others to believe Scotland was inherently weak in economic terms, while England was the strong partner in the Union. Many Scots continue to hold that erroneous view. All Scots should address themselves to the facts and set aside the myth.

The last five years have made manifest what was always true. It is not a case of some problem areas, such as Scotland, subsisting on a thriving southern centre. The *relative* prosperity of the English Home Counties survives for one principal reason — there is the seat of government and patronage and, incidentally, the core area for the one really big "pork barrel" in British public spending — the Defence Budget. Even that relative prosperity is a poor thing compared with similar centres in our Continental neighbours. The truth is that the whole United Kingdom is in decline and has been for a long, long time. The misconceived and naïve cold shower treatment of the Thatcher régime has served merely to expose the scale of the decline and the weaknesses more starkly than previous policies, which were really designed for a slow adjustment to the new poorer reality. We may come to thank Mrs Thatcher for that. For the parlous shape of the economy may serve to concentrate minds in Scotland on the possibilities of *our* recovery, instead of on the

116

demeaning obsessions with how we are doing compared with Merseyside or the South-East or the West Midlands of England. As Mrs Thatcher's policies drive home the lesson of decline, Tam Dalyell and others in the Labour Party are already trying to deflect Scottish attention from Scottish solutions by telling us that it is all a problem between north and south of the Trent. We must not fall for that one. Scotland can only survive and grow on a policy centred north of the Tweed.

In looking to the future, it is not Scotland but England which is found intrinsically the weaker of the two parties to the union. This comes out plainly in the difference between the two countries in the matter of endowment of natural resources. Of course, it is overly simplistic to suggest that copious natural resources are a *necessary* factor in producing economic success but it is hard to dispute that many of the world's richest and materially most successful economies are founded on a wealth of resources. Countries such as the USA, Canada and Australia enjoy a superabundance. Even in Europe, less obviously endowed, there are the farmlands of France, the forests of Finland and the gas of the Netherlands. Even Germany may be said to gain from her *location* because location is also a factor in the success of apparent "freaks" like Hong Kong. On any one of these measures, England stands out as weak. She has a relatively poor ability to feed herself. Even with the much increased agricultural output of recent years, owing nearly everything to massive artificial stimuli and subsidy, mainly via the EEC, the English population/food production equation is poor. Outside of coal she has little other natural resources to sustain one of the heaviest populated countries in the world.

Scotland by comparison has a much more favourable ratio of people to food production and, in addition, immense and potentially long-lasting indigenous energy resources. Only Norway in Europe comes close to being so favoured. It is a remarkable tribute to the political skill and manipulative ability of England's establishment that, in face of the facts, they have managed to persuade the Scots that what is untrue is true and what is true is untrue.

But all good things come to an end, and the bromide of economic lies upon which the Scots have been fed is now less effective. If there is to be a hope of Scottish economic recovery, then the prescription for our country must be very different from that for England. It is, as noted above, by no means the case that inherent weaknesses in natural resources on the English model is a bar to economic success. Japan, Taiwan and others demonstrate that quite clearly. But that weakness does impose conditions upon policy-making, designed to ensure that the raw materials and food deficit can be overcome by an economic and export performance in other goods and services. The policies that are demanded by the circumstances of inherent weakness are that priority for all investment must be towards the industrial export earnings sectors and in development. This the Japanese have done, particularly in the early days of recovery when they were forced to let social provision lag behind in the drive for industrial salvation.

England presents a very different picture to Japan. Once the Empire had gone and captive markets were no longer captive, the underlying decline of industry, which had been in train for almost 100 years, came to the surface. It has been a steep road downhill these past thirty years. Of course, there is no logical reason why England cannot do a Japan. But there are political and psychological barriers to the application of logic. There is also the breathing space of North Sea oil which, along with the Falklands adventure, has persuaded most people that there is no cause for panic: an England with its back to the wall will pull something out of the bag.

In reality, to stave off further decline and then build an export earning capaicty to maintain or even improve living standards in the long run, England needs a massive shift from consumption to investment, research and development. Massive is almost an understatement because the required investment needs to be of a magnitude greater than anything seen before in these islands. That shift from consumption to investment, especially at a time when the population is ageing and thus creating more demands for social services, can only mean a drop in the standard of living for a lengthy period. If this extraordinary level of investment took place, say, year upon year over a ten-year period, then we would see England's inherent weakness overcome. It will not happen. There will be no planned and socially just drop in the living standards of the people with a transfer of resources to investment. The decline will continue, the oil money will be misspent and the brunt of a continual drop in economic performance will fall upon around four million unemployed, the very low paid and a large section of the elderly who will rely entirely on state support. England will form into several socio-economic areas: in some the people will be generally well off and in others the levels of poverty will be high. At a rough guess, fifteen million people will be very poor.

England is economically weak and getting weaker by the year. It gives me no pleasure. But the fact cannot be avoided and it must be taken into account when we in Scotland are discussing the constitutional and economic relationship between ourselves and our southern neighbour.

England is caught in a post-empire syndrome of decline. All political parties there acknowledge the decline but there is no indication from even one of an understanding of the funda-mental weakness, the growing incapacity to overcome it and the demands on the people's sense of solidarity that a ten years' shift from consumption to investment would create. There are some in the Whitehall circles who know the true position but they are defeated by the politics of the country. English mass psychology does not admit of its basic economic weakness and the insularity of that nation allows them to avoid painful comparisons with the rest of the world. There is no chance of a political party in England being elected on a programme of overall reduced living standards as a precondition of economic recovery. So, instead of a planned and rational effort to reverse the cycle of history, all governments of whatever party will stumble along and economic failure will gather pace.

Let us pause for a moment to look at the extent of English

decline. This is what *Management Today* had to tell us in an editorial dated March 1983:

> All the signs are that the British economy is heading upwards out of the trough, lifted primarily by the consumer boom that has become traditional in pre-election years. When the immediate news (the monstrous unemployment figures apart) is getting steadily better, it's particularly sad to report that the long-term prognosis is getting worse.

Just how much worse was set out in a long article in the same edition by Simon Caulkin. He started off:

> Consider this familiar proposition: "Britain is a mainly industrial nation which pays its way by making a large surplus on its manufacturing trade to finance the import of food and raw materials, without which it cannot survive." Right? Wrong. As of 1982, the traditional model of the British economy, which has held ever since industrialisation itself, must be abandoned. Last year, for the first time ever, the one-time workshop of the world ran a deficit on its trade in those famous manufactures. The economy is thus at a watershed and no intelligent policy choices are possible, for government or managements, without recognising what has come to pass.

He goes on:

> Ahead is — what? "One last chance," says ex-BIM and Renold chairman Leslie Tolley, "to put things back on course." The only other alternative is a continuation of the present free fall into a kind of industrial black hole where deindustrialisation becomes so strong and so cumulative that there is no way back.

Mr Caulkin records that in all countries the share of GDP from manufacturing has fallen. For the OECD as a whole, it fell from 29.6% to 26.3% whereas in Britain the fall was from 32% to 21%, fully a third. Between 1958 and 1981, Britain's industrial output increased by only 49%. Belgium's rose 122%, France 144%, Germany 150%, and Italy 253%. The average for the original six-member EEC was 163%, over three times the British rate.

In Britain the workforce in manufacturing has fallen from 9 million in 1960 to 5.7 million now. Twelve years ago over two million vehicles were built and 827,000 of them exported. Imports then were around 20%. By 1982 vehicle production was down to only one million, exports shrunk to 395,000 and imports leapt to a 59% share of the domestic market. Mr Caulkin acknowledges "the plunge into deep manufacturing recession under Mrs Thatcher" but notes that even before 1979 there was a "colossal industrial investment shortfall to make good". Proof of this can be seen from a Written Answer to Gordon Wilson MP by the Minister for Trade and Industry:

## GROSS FIXED CAPITAL FORMATION: MANUFACTURING CONSTANT PRICES,[1] 1960 = 100

|  | Index | Year |
|---|---|---|
| Belgium | 164 | 1981 |
| Denmark | 93 | 1975 |
| F.R. Germany[2] | 168 | 1980 |
| France[3] | 256 | 1981 |
| Greece | 541 | 1981 |
| Ireland | 576 | 1980 |
| Italy[4] | 175 | 1980 |
| Netherlands[4] | 194 | 1981 |
| UK[5] | 78 | 1983 |
| USA | 337 | 1981 |
| Norway | 262 | 1981 |
| Sweden | 143 | 1981 |
| Korea | 2480 | 1979 |

1 1975 prices except Denmark, France and Greece (1970), FR Germany (1976) and UK (1980).
2 Later years include quarrying within manufacturing.
3 Mining, quarrying, manufacturing, electricity, gas and water.
4 Mining, quarrying, manufacturing, electricity, gas, water and construction.
5 Excludes assets leased from the service sector.

Source: UN Yearbook of National Accounts Statistics; OECD National Accounts; Business Statistics Office

(*Hansard* Written Answers, 27 June 1984)

The shortfall in investment is now so large that it is politically impossible to get the kind of consensus in England that is required to make it good. Will the majority of people in England vote for and continue to support a policy necessitating a sharp drop in living standards? They will not.

There is in Mr Caulkin's article a despairing note from NEDO director general Geoffrey Chandler: "The important thing is the complexity of causes. Depth in time, educational and cultural attitudes, design and quality, as well as price — it's all gone on so long, and everything is so interrelated, that symptoms become causes and vice-versa." The Scottish economy is of course embraced within Mr Caulkin's review, and the index released to Gordon Wilson. As the junior partner in the British state and its central decision-making, Scotland has followed England downhill and has been unable to take avoiding action despite our fundamental circumstances being different. It would be extremely difficult in a unitary state for the economy in one area, even one as easily defined in geographical and national terms as Scotland, to adopt different policies to those applying elsewhere. It has become impossible in Scotland because of the steady erosion of Scottish control over our public and private sectors and the total lack of political power to adopt alternative Scottish investment strategies. The position of Scotland within the United Kingdom, as the junior political partner of England, is simple and terrifying. We shall go down the industrial black hole first.

That should not happen. The fact that there is no hope of an English economic recovery does not mean that there is no hope north of the border. Whereas England is inherently weak, Scotland is inherently strong, self-sufficient in food and possessed of abundant indigenous resources of energy. What Scotland needs from external suppliers we can pay for.

There are many on the Scottish Left who, if they appreciate the truth about England's decline and the fact that the poor in that country will carry most burdens of that decline, feel guilty about any policy which would bring Scotland out of the English economic and political system. Those feelings are understand-able and laudable. The desire to help human beings in need and an uncomfortable feeling about rats leaving a sinking ship is legitimate. But it is a ship whose design and development has been kept firmly in English hands, Labour and Tory, devouring some of *our* best human talent over more than two centuries and which has been fuelled for the past decade by over £40 billion from oil drawn in Scottish waters. It is a ship skippered and crewed by people the English elected.

Responsibility for the English condition cannot be laid at Scotland's door. Any misconceived idea that England is our responsibility means increasing poverty among Scottish working people. The Scots cannot change English psychology, cannot make them face reality, cannot enforce policies upon them based on fairness and justice and cannot reverse the right-wing drift in southern policies. In short, the Scots cannot save the English and can only save themselves, if they will.

This assertion requires some elaboration. The English psychological problem is fatal ambivalence towards the attitudes and actions that need to be applied for success in the modern industrial and technical world, the aversion to reality and the refuge taken in beliefs about the efficacy of a system the rest of the world knows produces crazy policies. None of these are new phenomena. The genesis of the psychological flaw lay in the formative period of the industrial revolution when, instead of forging an unassailable lead and creating industrial dynamic, there took place what Professor Martin J. Weiner, of Rice University, USA, described as the "gentrification of the new business class".

In his book, *English Culture and the Decline of the Industrial Spirit — 1850-1980*, Weiner quotes Richard Cobden, whom he described as the "self-conscious spokesman of a bourgeois revolution writing with dismay about his troops deserting the cause". Cobden complained to a friend in 1863:

> We have the spirit of feudalism rife and rampant in the midst of the antagonistic development of the age of Watt, Arkwright, Stephen-

son! Nay, feudalism is every day more and more in the ascendant in political and social life. So great is its power and prestige that it draws to it the support and homage of even those who are the natural leaders of the newer and better civilisation. Manufacturers and merchants as a rule seem only to desire riches that they may be enabled to prostrate themselves at the feet of feudalism. How is it to end?

Weiner's own comments are:

As capitalism became landed gentlemen, JPs and men of breeding, the radical idea of active capital was submerged in the conservative ideal of passive property and the urge to enterprise faded beneath the preference for stability.

Professor Weiner makes a penetrating observation about the wilful neglect of science in the English public school system, which did so much to mould that nation's character:

The neglect of science rested upon an educational ideology. Its positive face was exaltation of the Greek and Roman classics as the basis of any liberal education. Its negative side was a fear of science as anti-religious, which sharply waned as the century drew on, and an association of science with vulgar industry, artisans and commercial utility, which did not diminish too readily. Head-masters, more or less equating the classics (together with Christianity, of course) with civilization and ideal mental training were eloquent in defence of a purely classical curriculum and they were backed up by most educated persons of note. No less a figure than Gladstone added his views: "What I feel is, that the relation of pure science, natural science, modern languages, modern history and the rest to the old classical training ought to be founded on a principle. . . . I deny their right to a parallel or equal position; their true position is ancillary and as ancillary it ought to be limited and restrained without scruple.

Restrained without scruple they were. By 1913, Germany was turning out 3,000 graduate engineers a year, whereas in Britain there were only 9,000 students altogether, with only 350 of them being in the sciences, technology and maths. The historian Corelli Barnett noted, in his *The Collapse of British Power* that: "From the very moment when British technology ceased to have the world's markets entirely to itself and had to face competition, its defeat was under way."

The gentrification process, and nostalgia for rural England, was not confined to the early years of the industrial revolution. Professor Weiner notes Arthur Bryant as saying, in 1936: "We may have become a nation of businessmen, but we are businessmen in spite of ourselves." He also quotes Graham Turner's view in 1969 that:

> While ICI men, not unnaturally, look upon themselves as something of an élite, they do not necessarily regard themselves as being an élite of business. "We think of ourselves as being a university with a purpose," said one of ICI's divisional chairmen. "We are very similar," said another senior executive, "to the Administrative Class of the Civil Service."

There is no respite from this depressing analysis by Weiner in the history or performance of the English Left. For example R. H. Tawney's dismissal of post-war concern with economic decline:

> When a Cabinet Minister declares that the greatness of this country depends upon the volume of its exports so that France, which exports comparatively little, and Elizabethan England, which exported next to nothing, are presumed to be pitied as altogether inferior civilisations, that is . . . the confusion of one minor department of life with the whole of life. . . . When the press clamours that the one thing needed to make this island an Arcadia is productivity, and more productivity, and yet more productivity, that is . . . the confusion of means with ends.

Professor Weiner does not of course suggest that the English Left is an exact mirror of the Right. For the Left he says the attraction is "the 'peasant' cultural tradition, the populist face of the rural myth". It is little wonder that with these deeply enhanced cultural attitudes that the public conduct and analysis supplied by the English political system has been no match for the reality of an inherently weak economy and the steep and open decline which became manifest once the empire was lost.

Senior politicians have shown no indication of understanding the English predicament. Each generation has gained office in a mood of optimism and has left it sad and disillusioned. Look at the record.

In the 1959 general election, on the crest of a consumer boom, Prime Minister Harold Macmillan told the people that they "had never had it so good". Macmillan is rightly regarded as one of the great English politicians, with a style and ability that set him above most others in an era of political heavyweights. But that subtle Edwardian mind was not capable of seeing that his late 1950s boom was the last fling before the lights dimmed as the power ebbed away. Put another way, the people had a ball eating the seed corn: the consumption which gave him and the people so much pleasure should have been invested to overcome the inherent weakness of the English economy. Reality finally undid Supermac.

Then it was 1964, and time for Harold Wilson to put an end to "thirteen wasted Tory years". Just thirteen you will note, not the 130 as it should have been said. Labour's 1964 election manifesto was brimming with vigour:

> The dying months of a frustrating 1964 can be transformed into the launching platform for the New Britain of the late 1960s and early 1970s.
>
> A New Britain—
>
> > **mobilising** the resources of technology under a national plan;
> >
> > **harnessing** our national wealth in brains, our genius for scientific invention and medical discovery;
> >
> > **reversing** the decline of thirteen wasted years;
> >
> > **affording** a new opportunity to equal and, if possible, surpass the roaring progress of other western powers while Tory Britain has moved sideways, backwards but seldom forward.
>
> The country needs fresh and virile leadership.
>
> Labour is ready. Poised to swing its plans into instant operation. Impatient to apply the New Thinking that will end the chaos and sterility.

126

Instant operation was postponed when Labour won with only three of a majority. But full opportunity seemed to present itself eighteen months later when in March 1966, Wilson beat Ted Heath in a landslide, giving Labour a majority of around 100. By July of that year the National Plan of recovery and economic growth was dead and its architect George Brown was on his long sad journey out of government. Labour's hopes were crushed by the reality of the inherent weakness of the English economy. You would never know this from listening to, or reading, Harold Wilson's speeches of those days. He was always promising the coming economic miracle, as were his Ministers. We were always just going to turn the corner. One night, I think from memory it was 1968, I saw Judith Hart, then a Cabinet Minister, interviewed from Rome. By a slip of the tongue she said, "We are just going round the bend." How true.

Wilson's government fell at the general election of 1970 and Ted Heath became Prime Minister. Unknown to us all, it was the very last chance for England to pull clear. As Professor Weiner points out, Heath seemed to have an instinctive grasp of the real underlying problem as had poor George Brown. In December 1969 Ted Heath described Britain as "a Luddite paradise . . . a society dedicated to the prevention of progress and the preservation of the status quo". In 1973 he was saying this:

> The alternative to expansion is not, as some occasionally seem to suppose, an England of quiet market towns linked only by trains puffing slowly and peacefully through green meadows. The alternative is slums, dangerous roads, old factories, cramped schools, stunted lives.

A prophet has no honour in his own land and Heath's administration ended in a shambles. Today, in 1985, he is still trying to make people face reality and is still crying in the wilderness.

From 1974 to 1979 we had the Wilson/Callaghan Labour government. The 1974 manifesto from Labour contained the radical promise to "irreversibly shift the balance of wealth and power to the working people and their families". That manifesto was drawn from the much larger policy document, Labour's *Programme 1973*, which promised a new economic strategy. But the old certainty was gone and a telling passage states:

> Indeed, it is now becoming clear that the British economy is so riven with deep structural faults that it is becoming increasingly difficult to manage at all — especially to combine full employment and a reasonable rate of growth with either a healthy balance of payments, or acceptable levels of inflation. Neither do we pretend to know all the answers. There is probably more uncertainty today about economic causes and effects, about economic relationships, about economic options than at any time since the thirties.

By July 1975 the Wilson government was facing its familiar crisis and from then on it lurched around from expedient to expedient. Wilson gave up and Jim Callaghan moved into Downing Street. The air was cleaner around Callaghan but the economic problems deepened and the Prime Minister took to making ridiculous speeches. He started forecasting a golden future around 1983. Labour were puzzled and beaten, taking refuge in delusion. There was no hint of understanding England's basic economic weakness and the Labour administration ended in confusion and defeat.

This brings us to Mrs Thatcher and her victory of 1979. As a so-called conviction politician, she is determined to reverse the decline of the post-war years. She blames the decline on the fudge and smudge of Butskellism and is thus herself guilty of failure to grasp the fact of inherent economic weakness in her own country. Mrs Thatcher's references to "Victorian values" betray her belief that in Victorian times there was an inner successful industrial dynamic. As Professor Weiner makes plain, it was in Victorian times that the industrial pass was sold. Once Mrs Thatcher has gone from office and her reign is put into perspective, many will come to realise that she has a good but narrow mind, fed by a tunnel vision and a blind patriotism which excludes an assessment of reality. Her administration is already losing its way on the major economic issue of how to turn around a decline arising from fundamental weakness. Like all her predecessors during the era of acute decline, she has placed her faith in fallacies, such as monetarism, Victorian values and wishful thinking.

She is not alone. On the 9th April 1984, the Chancellor of the Exchequer, Mr Nigel Lawson, informed the Third Cambridge Conference on International Energy that there was no cause for alarm about the future decline in North Sea oil revenue and the loss of self-sufficiency in energy which oil has delivered:

> Once oil production is past its peak, it is reasonable to expect that there will be some return to the traditional trade patterns of a surplus in manufacturing and invisibles offsetting deficits in food, basic material and eventually fuel.

Just how this miracle is to be achieved is, of course, not explained — except that is by one of those marvellous meaningless slogans that English Prime Ministers spout when the economic facts, such as four million unemployed and demoralising deindustrialisation, are too difficult to accept.

At the same time Nigel Lawson was relating future fables at Cambridge, Mrs Thatcher was being interviewed on BBC Panorama by Sir Robin Day. She told him she was busy creating a "go-getter society". She was, in the course of conversation, drawn into admitting that there had been a huge outflow of investment capital from Britain to other parts of the world. Over the period of her premiership £27 billion has gone this way. She thought this was a good thing. The lady was calm, proud and confident. Ignorance is bliss.

This essay has been concerned with giving Scots a proper view of the English economy, the myth about whose strength and superiority to our own has been so damaging. I have pointed out earlier that the Scots cannot change the English. Scotland is like a self-sufficient, small ship drawn along by a tow rope in the wake of the *Titanic*. We have been overawed by her size, her glamorous paintwork, sophistication, the bright lights, the open assertion by her passengers of their cultural class and their self-confidence. We believed the boasts of her designers and crew that she was the best-ever and unsinkable. Now the truth is out. She has hit the iceberg of reality, the cold waters of the present are drowning the nostalgic past, she is going down, down. The choice for us in Scotland is to either cut the rope which binds us to Titanic England, or go down with her.

*Chapter 7*

# DEMOCRATIC SOCIALISM: A SCOTTISH VIEW

Democratic Socialism is a child of modern society and so of relativist philosophy. It seeks the truth in any given situation, knowing all the time that if this be pushed too far it falls into error.

Its chief enemy is vacillation, for it must achieve passion in action in the pursuit of qualified judgements. It must know how to enjoy the struggle, while recognising that progress is not the elimination of struggle but rather a change in its terms.

Aneurin Bevan: *In Place of Fear*

IN THE BRITISH ISLES, democratic socialism is in disarray and the new Right has been winning the battle of ideas. It is not difficult to understand why this should be. During the era of economic expansion, from the mid-1950s to the early 1970s, socialists believed that economic growth would allow them to change society without upsetting any section, including the capitalist establishment. The old socialist analysis about capitalism containing contradictions that lead to inevitable crises was pushed aside. Not only were the swinging sixties permissive in the social sense, they were the locust years in the intellectual life of the socialist movement. So much so that when the latest crisis of capitalism did arrive, when the West could no longer filch Arab oil at ridiculously low prices, democratic socialism was unprepared and short on ideas. As the crisis developed, socialist thought and action entered a purely negative phase, particularly those elements anchored to the Labour Party. First there was simple resistance to the Selsdon Park policies of the Heath administration of 1970-74. When Heath took a U-turn and boosted economic growth in an effort to escape from post-war decline there was even less reason for fresh thinking because Labour saw its resistance campaign as having worked. The unfortunate John Davies, Heath's Secretary of State for Industry, received an ironic standing ovation from Labour MPs when he announced his department's expansion programme.

Then between 1974 and 1979, with Labour back in government but struggling, there was a period of self-satisfaction resting upon past achievements. Take Roy Hattersley, now Deputy Leader of the Labour Party, delivering the Barnet Shrine Lecture at Queen Mary College, London, in 1978:

> The ameliorators' achievement has been very substantial. They have concentrated the party's mind on real issues — actually doing things that are within our power rather than dreaming of progress beyond us. They have created what Sir Keith Joseph calls "the socialist ratchet" and have kept that piece of machinery in good working order. In the past much of each Labour government's policy has survived electoral defeat because it is advocated in terms which were neither doctrinal nor polemical.

To be fair, Roy Hattersley also said that Labour required an ideological basis for its activities and noted that "without a theoretical impetus even the zeal to ameliorate will begin to fade". But for this theoretical impetus he drew largely upon Tony Crosland's *The Future of Socialism*, written in 1956, which has become the foundation work for all those who believed that capitalist growth would continue without interruption and thus offer the chance of painless change.

But let us come back to the Hattersley boast about the socialist ratchet, which was thought to place past achievement beyond the ability of subsequent governments, however right wing, to attack and destroy. This revealed a remarkably static view of society and discounted the importance of political theory and debate. Somehow the ratchet had taken education, National Health Service, housing, social security and employment policies to a safe consensus position. This negative thinking was to prove no match for the positive right-wing ideological assault Mrs Thatcher unleashed on all post-war nostrums, pinning the blame on Labourism and Butskellism for the indisputable decline in British economic performance. She found it easy to slip the catch and reverse the ratchet.

The negativity is still with us. Take a clear example from the darling of the British Labour Left, Tony Benn. Interviewed by Peter Jay in Channel 4's Week in Politics on 6 January 1984, he was asked: "What specifically is democratic socialism as a policy?" Benn replied:

> Well it's a very theoretical question because the Labour movement was brought into being to defend the interests of working people and their families. And it was set up by the trade union movement. It became a socialist party in 1918 officially and its task is to try to protect people against probably the most brutal and cruel government we've seen in my lifetime, a government that has deliberately created four million unemployed, that is deliberately destroying the National Health Service and our educational system, that has allowed an American President we don't control to bring missiles here which he can fire from our territory without our consent, that is now engaged in a death struggle with the Market, the Common Market, which has been a disaster for Britain. And therefore what the Labour Party's tried to do in the *Manifesto* and the *Programme* — and no doubt we shall develop it further between now and the next election — is to identify practical things we can do to get people back to work, to have a big housing programme, to develop our educational system on a more comprehensive basis, to assist pensioners, to deal with the practical problems and above all to see that we're not dragged into a nuclear war by an irresponsible and dangerous President who at the moment has got his own nuclear missiles in Britain. Now that's what the Labour Party's about and theoretical arguments about socialism go on because it's a very interesting subject.

That rambling answer is shown in full, to avoid accusations of selective quotes. What Tony Benn described was not the theoretical basis of democratic socialism: that is, the philosophical and practical qualities that mark it as different, say, from radical liberalism, or, more important, the Marxist socialism of Eastern Europe. Nor did he describe what it is as a policy. He tells us what Labour is against, the effect of Conservative government policies and that Labour's task between 1984 and the next election "is to identify practical things we can do to get people back to work" and so on. Those last words are the everyday currency of political propaganda and go nowhere near the root of the question put by Peter Jay.

Why Benn should fail to answer that question is best described by Gavin Kitching in his book *Rethinking Socialism* where he categorises Benn and others as Romantic anti-capitalists:

> They are essentially resisters, rather than revolutionaries, because, though they lament and attack capitalism's impact upon the lives of working people past and present, they really have very few ideas, or indeed no ideas at all, about how, and in what precise respects, capitalism can be changed.

Roy Hattersley's ameliorators and Tony Benn's resisters do not represent democratic socialism. So what is it? The phrase "democratic socialism" had to be invented in order to distance the West European socialist movement from the socialism that emerged in Stalin's Soviet Union and ultimately in the buffer states set up by the power of the Red Army. Soviet socialism certainly caused a transfer from capitalist ownership to state ownership and brought the means of production, exchange and control into non-private hands. The cost in human suffering was enormous: the intellectual, scientific and artistic life of the people was twisted to serve the declared views of the Communist Party, which became the new power élite. At the heart of Soviet socialism lies the belief that social change should be engineered at any price and that democracy — which ultimately means the right of people to be wrong as things are seen by their government — is a hindrance to progress. West European socialists believed, at least in theory, in the public ownership of the means of production, exchange and control: this much they shared with the Communists. What they did not share was the kind of hatred that could fuel Stalinist purges against the kulaks and small capitalists. Nor did they share the messianic certainty with which Communists addressed complex problems about world economic and social development. The central feature of Communist theory and practice, that leadership of the people would be exercised through an élitist dictatorship, was anathema to these non-Communist socialists. So, a clear difference existed but there was a need to formalise it. There was a need to protect Western socialism's reputation as a liberalising creed and to remove anxiety in the mind of the Western public that a vote for socialism in their own country would not inevitably lead to the four o'clock knock in the morning, destruction of free thinking and speaking and the imposition of a permanent dictatorship. The formalisation of the difference came in the term democratic socialism.

For me the main difference between democratic socialism and the Soviet form is that the former believes you cannot build a truly socialist society without first converting a significant proportion of society to socialist ethics and ideals, thus shifting the spectrum of opinion leftwards, whereas the latter seeks to accomplish socialism by coercion, the generation of controlled propaganda and, if necessary, by armed force.

Democratic socialism seeks to change some of the fundamentals in the character of the people. Specifically, those aspects of our nature which can so easily set person against person: greed, the desire to acquire power over others and a propensity to exploit human need for private gain. It is a creed that can only achieve its objective of a change in the character of humankind by an intellectual conversion which leads people to accept and support the higher morality inherent in the socialist ethic and do so voluntarily. That ethic seeks to tame market forces and insert the criterion of human need into the consideration of policy as a first priority. It seeks forms of government and extensions of democracy and responsibility that draw people together and enables them to place human need and common good as the principal objectives which an economic system must serve before all others. The socialist ethic seeks to give the individual protection for his individualism by making sacrosanct his or her rights to free thought, free speech and a private life. In return the individual is expected to have, and exercise, obligations towards improving the spiritual, cultural, material and civilised state of the community.

The ethic is also concerned with equality but this is something that requires elaboration, even some pedantry. Nothing leaves the democratic socialist more open to misrepresentation and attack by opponents than socialism's attachment to the concept of equality. There is a widespread anxiety about what socialist equality will really mean. It is sometimes misrepresented as the politics of envy, a desire to get even with the rich by reducing them to a low level of standards and income, creating a kind of sour happiness in society based on the feeling that although everyone is down, no one is on the up and up. There is a general belief that within socialism is a desire to level downwards and that somehow we socialists wish to iron out every wrinkle of character and beautiful curve on the human face, making it bland and uninteresting. It has to be acknowledged that some of the hard, hate-filled language spouting from the mouths of some Labour ultra-leftists lends credence to the general unease with which people respond to socialist equality. We cannot argue that all people are created equal because that is demonstrably false if we are talking about the gifts, talents and personalities of people. If, however, we argue that socialism's task is to create equal rights of access to high quality housing, to income levels that allow of an expansive life, to education, to a good health service, to work and job satisfaction and to care in old age or infirmity, then we are defining the concept of equality in a way that recognises the reality of differences between people but seeks to meet needs that are basic to all.

In a most interesting and thoughtful speech to a Labour Party meeting in Newcastle on 29 July 1983, Roy Hattersley has this to say on the subject:

> The vision of a more equal society which should inspire and sustain the Labour Party is not a pretence that we are all equal. *It is the insistence that society should be organised in a way which reduces rather than emphasises the intrinsic differences between individuals.* It is the conviction that today our laws, our habits and our prejudices all accentuate the divisions in society and that we should create new laws and new institutions which draw society together.
>
> (Roy Hattersley's own emphasis.)

I differ from Roy Hattersley. If human society is to retain its dynamic and fulfil its potential, the great array of talent and skill to be found in the intrinsic differences between people must be encouraged to flourish. A society should organise itself so that the *consequences* of intrinsic difference and their interplay in economic, scientific and cultural life are wholly beneficial and not harmful to the general good; that the differences are not used to build economic and social class barriers, that everyone's constructive contribution to society is openly proclaimed as valuable and that rewards for working, giving one's talents, are based on a sensible and fair system which does not create enormous disparities between one group and another.

A democratic socialist should not fear or try to reduce or suppress emphasis on intrinsic differences. These differences are a matter for rejoicing. They mean that million upon millions of people each give something of themselves, something unique to them to the great pool of ability available to the human race. The task of democratic socialism is to establish a new social order of principles which take away the need for people to employ their intrinsic talents, or acquired skills, to carve out a special superior position for themselves as opposed to others. When a new social order of principle is established, then talent can have a free rein without posing a threat to social harmony and justice. One of the great problems that socialists face in trying to get people to listen, never mind convert them, is that all too often we give the impression that a socialist society will be dull, a place where even the rainbows will exhibit only shades of grey, spontaneity will be officially discouraged, humour will be unwelcome and all minds will concentrate only on "serious" matters. A kind of permanent puritanism. Of course that is a parody. It is unfair. But it is the kind of imagery that supporters of capitalism employ against us. When Roy Hattersley speaks of reducing emphasis on the differences between people, he opens democratic socialism to the accusation that we "want to make everyone the same" and that socialism aims to produce equality through grinding down talent until we all meet in mediocrity.

If we are to succeed with the intellectual conversion of people to the idea and ideals of socialism, then we must state explicitly that we seek a society which positively welcomes variety, contending schools of art and culture, creativity, experimentation, laughter and the excitement inherent in each new generation's birth and achievements. It is also important to explain that democratic socialism, unlike Soviet socialism, eschews dogmatic assertions that socialists have a monopoly of knowledge on what makes the world tick. There should be no body of dogma in democratic socialism, no high priests at whose feet of clay we are forced to worship and no arrogant assumption that our socialism gives us a "scientific" edge on everyone else concerned about human development. Democratic socialists believe their way is best because our objective is to change and civilise the nature of humankind. But we must be honest and admit our problems in meeting that objective.

Aneurin Bevan's *In Place of Fear* points out that democratic socialism is gradualist, undogmatic and that it is faced not with one absolutely certain response to every major issue but always has a number of options and must always bear the pain of choice between what is practicable and what is most desirable. As Bevan puts it: "Its chief enemy is vacillation for it must achieve passion in action in the pursuit of qualified judgements." That is not a revolutionary creed. Bevan's comments have no connotations of the cataclysmic. Democratic socialism places most weight on civilised behaviour. It is not fuelled by blind hate for the wrongs mankind has done but is concerned to see that man's inhumanity to man is not repeated throughout the ages to come. It is a gradualist creed because its aim is to change minds and, while it is an easy task to seize the body of a human being or hold a whole nation under subjection, it is a much slower process to alter minds by patient persuasion in a pluralist society, especially when minds have been conditioned by the history of Lord and Servant in feudal times and recently by the experience of Boss and Worker in capitalist industrialist society. Mao Tse Tung claimed that political power grew out of the barrel of a gun. Democratic socialism believes that the human mind and the human soul are, when fired by a desire to create justice, capable of generating a power far superior and more enduring than anything that comes from a gun.

Democratic socialism does not hold out the promise of a short-cut to the promised land. It is more of a philosophy than a blueprint for change. It is a philosophy, moreover, that can only give a crude guide to the many paths and trails made by unpredictable humankind on its journey through modern times. However, because it lacks a code of absolutes and has no shelfful of "scientific" forecasts about how and when the millennium will dawn, it is wrong to think that democratic socialism is a soft option for those who want change but are squeamish about the kind of blood on the hands of the Kremlin.

The democratic way is a hard road. It calls for qualities of character, stamina, determination, tolerance, reason and audacity. But above all, it requires solid commitment to progress through persuasion and education so that new principles of individual and community conduct take root and grow to strengthen socialist action by making changes by consent of the people. What makes it a particularly hard road is that the democratic socialist is required to accept defeat, to see injustice and poverty stalk the land, and to witness the re-emergence of cruel disregard for the weak and vulnerable, which has been the chief characteristic of the Conservative government elected in 1979 — all without falling into the temptation of seeking forcible change through violence. *Democratic socialism does not rule out strong challenge to a capitalist establishment. Techniques for effective industrial action in support of political objectives and concerted extra- and intra-parliamentary activity must be developed and employed in the struggle between socialist aims and entrenched capitalist power.* Our kind of socialism has to rouse, yet control, passion. It is not easy but it is a better way than to extinguish opposition by the gun, fired with hatred.

What has all this to do with Scotland? Ours is a country which is heavily influenced by the basic idea, and several schools, of socialism. That is one reason why Scotland, unlike England, has proved so resistant to the right-wing values which Mrs Thatcher has been so successful in propounding south of the border. Because of our social and economic history, in which socialism played such a key rôle, Scots still hold firmly to ideas about common care and concern for humanity and the need for a sense of community solidarity. There is, therefore, a gulf growing between Scotland and England. Fewer and fewer Scots are able to escape from the conclusion that if our values are to prevail in our civil government, we shall need to seek self-government. That immediately raises the question of what kind of Scotland such a self-governing entity would be and that question can only be answered by reference to major influences on attitudes and potential political development. Socialism is not the only influence at work of course. Calvinism and Scots Catholicism (quite different from its English counterpart) have a profound influence on matters other than the purely religious; so too do the values of those parts of Scotland where we find the small sturdy towns of the North East and the Borders, where divisions in class terms are less sharp and painful than in the industrial conurbations. But there is no dispute that socialism and its

140

development are a major factor in how we think and act now and will continue to be of crucial importance. It follows that which school of socialist thought emerges as supreme can in turn influence the attitude of the whole people, including non-socialists, to the idea of self-government. It is important per se that Scottish socialists should found themselves on the democratic school but we must also recognise the legitimate interest of our fellow citizens in our thoughts and intentions.

What I have attempted to set out is that at the heart of democratic socialism lies the belief in change by persuasion and intelligent political campaigning which sharpens the focus on socialism's superiority to what MacDiarmid correctly identifies as capitalism's "senseless and wanton quality", its urge to material aggrandisement of the relatively few by the exploitation of the many. Democratic socialism does believe that it *is* possible to produce profound irreversible change in the nature and form of society and that the permanence of change can only be guaranteed if it is built upon the intellectual conversion of the people. It is this school of socialism which represents the mainstream Left in Scotland and it is this kind of socialism that would develop and enlarge its influence in a self-governing Scotland. It does not seek to promote class war or seek a warlike victory. Unlike large countries, where big populations of fifty million and above make it easy for pure theory and geographical division to work on raw feelings, with alienation increased through lack of all but minimal human social contact, Scotland is a small and remarkable homogeneous nation.

There *are* class differences and divisions of wealth in Scotland but we are not a hate-filled nation. In a big country, it is easy to hate across the class barriers in the abstract. That is not possible to any significant degree in a small country where people and personalities are fairly widely known and evaluated as human beings rather than as representatives of this or that class of special interest.

Now, I don't want to overstate the position. The Industrial

Revolution has left its mark on the working class who suffered principally at the hands of native Scottish bosses. But I have found that today's working class, while conscious of their history at the hands of capitalism, have an ability to look objectively at someone who is on the other side of the labour v. capital struggle. Similarly, in the ranks of capital, you find men and women who through contact with individuals in the Labour movement and a general appreciation of the whole make-up of Scottish society, can understand what makes a shop steward tick and a socialist seek to change society. It is interesting to note that just as Scotland as a whole has resisted the Thatcher ideology, many in the ranks of Scottish business and industry can be heard, audibly, expressing deep reservations and often outright opposition to policies of high unemployment and cuts in social services. While there are some in Scottish society who are immune to the suffering around them and some who respond with a bitterness that eats into their souls, most Scots have a remarkable tolerance in class terms.

A Scotland that is self-governing will not be free of tension and tussle; nor will it escape from the inherent conflict that must exist between capital and labour. Scottish capitalism is by no means dead and any economic recovery will provide it with new recruits and new strengths, and its differences with labour will create industrial and political activity as the broad mass of the people struggle to assert their rights to control the forces that dominate the economy.

It is how the contest is conducted, its rules, the motives of those involved, their aims and their methods which are important. Because it seeks conversion of the intellect as a precondition for real advancement and the creation of an ethos in which socialist ideas become part of the pattern of life, there is no place for class-war rhetoric or practice in democratic socialism. War is about destruction. Conversion is about development and construction. Democratic socialism should have a special appeal to the people of Scotland, not because we are intrinsically kinder than others, but because our history, experience, size and homogeneity makes us more open to its salient features — responsibility and obligations to the community, the sense of solidarity it creates, the unremitting effort to harness economic forces to serve the people and its freedom from hatred. Democratic socialism applied in Scotland will shift the balance of wealth and power to working people and their families: it would fail if it failed to do that. It will cause those who hold disproportionate power to relinquish it for the common good. It will encourage the organisation of labour and will have a bias towards the rights of working people. And it will do all this in a sensitive and humane fashion, mindful that taking power from one group is not a licence to humiliate or wound people from that group. People, who are not socialists, are first and foremost our fellow citizens and their dignity and well-being must be taken into account in all that we do. Humanity and socialism are indivisible.

*Chapter 8*

# AN INESCAPABLE CHOICE FOR THE SNP: THE CLASS ISSUE

The SNP is a radical party with a revolutionary aim.
Donald Stewart, MP: SNP Conference 1984

No political party can possibly lead a great revolutionary movement to victory unless it possesses revolutionary theory and a knowledge of history and has a profound grasp of the practical movement.
Mao Tse Tung: *The Little Red Book*

DONALD STEWART WAS, of course, talking about a different kind of revolution than Mao Tse Tung. The latter saw power as emerging only from the barrel of a gun and, given the non-democratic history of China, he was no doubt correct in his context. Scottish tradition is different from that of China and we share with the English and Welsh a veneration for power emerging from the ballot box.

There has only been one armed attempt at revolution in modern Scottish times. In 1820, when under the banner "Scotland Free or a Desert", weavers and other workers led by Baird, Hardie and Wilson made an abortive effort to overthrow what they saw as an alien, corrupt, undemocratic English government of Scotland. The three leaders and many others shot in the streets paid the price of failure with their lives but their martyrs' blood fertilised no political soil. Some remembered them but most of the Scottish population, includ-

144

ing the ranks of organised labour, have been largely ignorant of the heroism and sacrifice of 1820. Happily, this ignorance is being dispelled by the vigorous efforts of the 1820 Society but it has taken 165 years for the significance of Baird, Hardie and Wilson to dawn on Scottish political activists.

Those who have lingered in folk memory are all drawn from the mainstream democratic tradition: the Scottish Chartists who lobbied and demonstrated for the franchise, the early trade unionists who defied laws against combination or, like Keir Hardie, faced a stoning in mining villages when trying to organise trade unions, Jimmie Maxton and his Clydesiders or John McLean who preached a fundamental socialism but submitted himself to the hustings. It is, therefore, to the democratic revolution that Donald Stewart referred. One that requires a great sea of change of opinion, expressed ultimately by a cross on a ballot paper, a new opinion so profound and determined that it cannot be shifted from its new course — to overthrow an old order and impose a new constitutional policy.

Notwithstanding the difference in the two types of revolution encompassed by the opening quotes, there is an important element in Mao's thinking which is essential to any successful attempt at *any* kind of revolution. Those who seek the objective of change must be guided by theory, based upon a hard analysis of the power structure of society, the forces which promote and defend the status quo, the forces for change and the level of their development and how the latter can be harnessed and employed to reach the stated objective. Any revolutionary statement of intent which has no foundation in theory is empty rhetoric. A source of cheap applause at a conference, it can take neither party nor people one step forward which is why it passes out of the collective memory soon after the clapping stops. This is the case with the SNP. But it would be wrong to say that the fault lies with Donald Stewart. The fault is party-wide. The SNP is a party with a revolutionary intent, without a theory to back it up. That is why the party goes adrift, with large sections actually talking about waiting around until the next wave of nationalism lifts it up for all to see and admire once again. I don't dispute that there can indeed be waves of national feeling which, frustrated and angry at lack of movement in the British party structure, turns to the SNP to shock and warn our rulers about going too far in neglect of our interests. But, as the fate of the SNP between 1974's high point and the electoral disaster of 1979 showed, such protest support can ebb as quickly as it flows. If it is to succeed in its aims, then the SNP must carry through a democratic revolution and a prerequisite is electoral support set in concrete in its favour. Getting electoral support as a temporary phenomenon is always possible. Holding that support through thick and thin is what really counts because the trial of strength with the British establishment will not be confined to one election but will continue long after the successful polling day as they try one stratagem after another to bring the march to self-government grinding to a halt.

During the majority of its fifty-one years, the SNP has been dominated by what is known as the traditionalist wing. People who openly argue that matters such as class in industrial society and ideology are foreign inventions imported to Scotland as a means of dividing and ruling us, with no relevance whatever to our condition. They wish to avoid all serious debate and division on economic and social issues until independence is won. Then, and only then, will it be sensible and legitimate for Scots to quarrel on domestic policy. In their view the labels of Left and Right are made in England and are meant to confuse and divert Scottish opinion from the goal of independence. The old guard traditionalist leadership, led by Robert McIntyre, profoundly influenced the huge influx of new members after Winnie Ewing's triumph at the Hamilton bye-election. This became a new generation of political activists, many of them without previous experience of politics; and they were easy to shape and mould in the old image. Keith Webb, in his *The Growth of Nationalism in Scotland*, published in 1977, said this:

> The ideals central to the SNP are beliefs in decentralisation, the
> rightness of economic development and local democracy *and in the*

existence of a distinctive and non-doctrinaire "Scottish Way" in politics. . . .

Thus, while it is true that the modern nationalist programme is very different from the vague and wordy statements of the early party, the policies of the present party can be seen as the application and extension of ideas implicit in the beliefs of the founders. In spite of very great change there remains a thread of ideological continuity. . . . (Emphasis added.)

It would have been more accurate for Keith Webb to have written that the thread of continuity was in eschewing ideology. That small criticism apart, there is no doubt that he captures the outlook of the SNP as it stood in 1977, shaped by the traditionalists. Even more revealing was Keith Webb's explanation of an important element in the party's apparent success in the mid-seventies:

The responsible image is heightened by other factors. The party leadership in the main tend to be very respectable figures, differing little in socio-economic status from the leadership groups in other parties. The party chairman, indeed, is a strong churchman and chartered accountant. . . . There is very little about the SNP leadership which is likely to frighten the potential voter and much that will reassure him. . . .

From these words of the SNP's most admiring biographer, we see the traditionalist SNP as devoid of theory, unaware of the true revolutionary nature of its task, fitting snugly into the norms of respectability laid down by its enemies.

The weakness of the traditionalists is that they draw inspiration from events in medieval times, regarding Wallace and Bruce as *the* outstanding figures in the whole history of Scotland. Admittedly, the Scottish wars of independence fought by Wallace and Bruce in the late thirteenth and early fourteenth centuries do inspire admiration for the courage and valour of Wallace and the leadership, statesmanship and diplomatic, as well as martial, skills of Bruce. Their deeds have transmitted down through the ages not only a thrill of achievement but a force, a potent inescapable call of duty, for the Scots to hold themselves as being a distinct nation. But much has happened since the battle of Bannockburn in 1314 which does not seem to excite and stimulate the traditionalists. Since then we have been through the Highland Clearances, the Industrial Revolution, the struggle for democracy and trade union rights. The Industrial Revolution, with the rise of capitalism and the creation of modern productive capacity and an industrial working class, formed the crucible in which present-day Scotland was cast. The steam that turned the first wheels of the new age cauterised the past and blew us into a new era which produced a new set of challenges and internal conflict between Scots workers and employers. It is that new age and its legacy of class, clashing ideologies and opposed vested interests that the traditionalists turn away from — back to Bannockburn where the issues seem simple and non-divisive.

When the SNP was on the fringe of Scottish politics, as it was from its formation in 1934 to 1967, the traditionalist refusal to face the realities of class, and Left and Right, hardly mattered. But after the Hamilton bye-election, and especially between 1974 and 1979, when the party had eleven MPs, it found that the magical all-round Scottishness did not exist.

Issues that divided capital from labour and Left from Right intruded upon the world of traditionalist make-believe. The litmus test was the Bill introduced by the Labour government in 1975 to nationalise the shipyards. Labour had a narrow majority and there was genuine doubt whether the Bill, which suffered a rough legislative passage, would ever become an Act. The Bill was regarded by a majority of all Scottish workers, not just the shipyard workers, as a vital measure. After generations of shipyard workers had been shamelessly used and abused by private owners, the yards were to pass into public ownership. That would produce a new management, and give workers and their unions an inside track through which to press their views on investment, manpower policy, wages and conditions. Public ownership meant different standards, better standards, of consideration and treatment. Above all it brought an opportunity for trade unions to directly influence the final decision-makers, the government. The Scottish workers were not stupid. They did not see nationalisation as a panacea. For years they had been warning about the consequences of ship-building decline and all were aware of the painful adjustments that changing world circumstances would impose. But nationalisation gave the workers an edge, some chance to influence their own lives, which private ownership never could.

In the knife-edge parliamentary situation, the SNP looked as though it could prove decisive. At a critical period in the passage of the legislation the SNP cast its votes against the Bill. The SNP explained that they wanted a separate Scottish division of British Shipbuilders. On the face of it that was a reasonable tactical position for the party to adopt. In fact it was an error to justify a vote against the Bill on grounds that no such separate division was conceded. The invocation of the purely Scottish dimension, around which the SNP no doubt expected to gather support from all sections of Scotland's supposedly classless society, cut no ice with the workers. What was at stake was either a victory for Scottish workers in alliance with workers in the south, or a victory for Scottish bosses allied with their kind in England and Wales. Given their history and their needs, Scottish workers could see it no other way. The SNP was on the spot. They were either for Them or Us. Protest as they did that they were refusing to get drawn into an English inspired Left versus Right argument, the SNP found itself playing a key rôle right at the heart of the issue. The most detailed knowledge of the battle of Bannockburn and the most eloquent cry for us all to "think Scottish" and assert that we were all of one body, one mind, one nation and one interest was useless. The party of democratic revolution had been fed on fairytales. It had no theoretical understanding of the forces at work in Scottish society, and so fell inevitably into practical error. They gifted the Labour Party a stick to beat across the head of every nationalist candidate from then until the General Election of 1979.

149

The General Election of 1979, when the SNP lost nine seats, brought different reactions within the SNP. The traditionalists saw no fault in their previously held position. Seeing no need for theory, they claimed the defeat had arisen because they were tricked by the unionist parties into supporting a devolution Bill, thus diverting both the party and the public from a concentration on the idea of independence. A plague was called down upon those who would not sing the old empty tunes. It was to be "Independence nothing less" that was to be drummed into the Scottish earhole. Not surprisingly, in the real world where Mrs Thatcher's right-wing government was walloping the working people with attacks upon the welfare state and the destruction of employment security, the Scots proved deaf to the traditionalist noise. There were those within the party who even before the election of 1979 had started to push their thinking deeper and nearer to what was the reality of Scottish society. Some of them joined the '79 Group (which was subsequently banned), but not all. In the six years after 1979, there has been a deliberate attempt by many people to introduce the need for theory to the SNP, and to start up and sustain a debate.

Slowly, but surely, the party is at last swinging round to the recognition that political analysis is a precondition of successful action. But there is still some way to go and little time if we are to take Scotland forward to self-government before the remaining fifteen years of this century expire. The main thrust of strategy must be to maintain the party in a Left position and to develop its thinking to the point where our collective response to any issue is guided by philosophy and instinct, that puts us unerringly on the side of labour and progressive opinion no matter the issue that lands unexpectedly before us. Some members of the SNP will say "but we are a left of centre party, just look at our policies". True. When each individual policy of the party is examined, whether it be on land ownership, the need to reconstruct the economy through public sector action, housing, the health service, education, or the rights of trade unions, they clearly place us left of centre.

I shall argue that any objective analysis of Scottish society will result in the SNP remaining firmly in a left of centre position, and developing its thinking to the point where our collective response to any issue is guided by philosophy and instinct, that puts us unerringly on the side of working people and progressive opinion no matter the issue that lands unexpectedly before us. The theory on which forward movement is based must look not so much at activists but at the institutions through which Scotland functions and the vested interests they serve. It is difficult for political activists to see other people as different from themselves. Activists are motivated by a passion to see society order itself in the way that they wish. They have a willingness to engage in personal effort to the point of sacrifice to achieve certain goals of structure, order and moral conduct. The activist assaults the rest of society with his ideas and ideals and plans for this and that. The enthusiasm, commitment and energy of the activist *can* light fires among people and these fires do generate great winds of human emotion in which almost everyone can be carried along. That emotion is merely fuel. The *engines* of change, whose movement or immobility are crucial, are institutions that speak and act for the groups of vested interests into which we are all organised. If political activists pay no regard to institutional interests, believing they can all be by-passed by the collective power of a people enthused at an individual level, then they will meet failure. The fuel of emotion, like petrol spilled and set alight at random, will run and burn freely, even spectacularly, but does eventually evaporate. Ignited in the combustion chambers of institutional machinery, the fuel produces movement of significance. It is this that the traditionalists could never understand.

It is when one looks at institutional Scotland, at the vested interests, that the imperative of a left of centre position emerges. The concept of independence rightly excites SNP members who want to shake off the intellectual handicap of being run by another people. But that concept is measured more prosaically by the institutions who judge whether it will benefit or harm their interests. Usually, institutions dress up their position as being concerned with some broad duty but at heart they take a narrow view of what is good or bad for them. This is a realist's, not a cynic's, view. The romanticisation of the American and French revolutions came after the events. These great episodes were caused, sustained and won by institutions whose perceived interests could no longer be served by the old order. It was similar in Zimbabwe where the desire for land on the part of rural black people was employed by Mugabe's forces, in particular, to build and sustain a base from which to maintain pressure on the Smith régime. In South Africa in 1985, we saw the commercial and industrial vested interests of whites, under threat of black economic boycotts and external financial sanctions, press for changes in apartheid. When white industrialists met the African National Congress it was not out of a new-found respect for coloured human beings, but a process of looking after themselves.

In all of the above examples, people moved by ideals, willing and able to argue and agitate, were important. They prepared the moral ground upon which the institutional interests could step when action suited their needs and purposes. When change does not suit, then no amount of pulling, shoving and exhortation to patriotism will engage institutions in a forward gear. Indeed they will resist. This lesson was hammered home to the SNP in 1978 when the Parliamentary Group and others provoked the Associated Scottish Life Offices into the open:

> I was horrified to read in your issue of June 30 of the totally unwarranted attack made by Mr Robert Shirley, the prospective SNP candidate for Edinburgh South, on Mr David Donald, general manager of the Standard Life Assurance Company, when he accused him of "abusing his position out of political prejudice".
>
> I have been on the receiving end of a similar attack by an SNP MP and it would now seem that when they are confronted with statements which disagree with their views, SNP policy is not to try to answer the arguments put forward but to accuse the person concerned of political bias — a typical political trick.
>
> A report on all the possible effects on the Scottish Life offices of

separatism for Scotland has been prepared by the Associated Scottish Life Offices and discussed at length with the SNP and when Mr Donald suggested that in certain circumstances Standard Life might be forced to move its head office to England, he was simply pointing out what could happen to all Scottish Life offices if Scotland had a separate currency.

Life offices pay their expenses out of loadings in the premiums they collect. About 80 per cent of the loadings received by Scottish Life offices came from England and thus would be paid in English pounds but, because they have their head offices in Scotland, about 70 per cent of their expenses would have to be paid in Scottish pounds. It doesn't require much financial acumen, though obviously a little more than appears to be possessed by certain SNP politicians, to see that if the Scottish pound appreciated against the English pound then the time could arise when a Scottish Life office would have to move its head office to England.

Incidentally, the same arguments apply to any kind of business operating from a Scottish base whose sales are predominantly south of the border. Whether or not the Scottish pound were to appreciate against the English pound we have no way of knowing, but have not the SNP gone to great pains to assure us that it would?

Life offices normally try to avoid referring to matters of a political nature . . . there must be a wide divergence of political views among their policy-holders. . . . However, when the interests of these policy-holders are being threatened by politicians then I think that they would be failing in their duty if they did not tell them so.

W. Proudfoot, Chairman,
Associated Life Offices
(Letter to *The Scotsman*, 7 July 1978)

There in the last sentence, by use of the word "duty" is manufactured the moral position from which an institution can baldly state its narrow view. The extensive quote from that letter is by no means an attack on the Life Offices as being greedy and full of self-interest. Far from it. There is a legitimacy to that institution's position and its guiding rules. It could not be expected to support Scottish independence unless its interests were to be served by such a course. The letter is quoted in full, because it is a first-class exposition of the points I am seeking to make.

Scotland is, of course, made up of more than Life offices,

banks, building societies and investment groups. Other institutional interests are to be found in the world of industry, the public services and in the social and political organisations which embody the values created by working people. My argument is that, while we may be able to pacify the Life Offices and the banks and render them less hostile to independence, especially if it is to be achieved through continuing membership of the European Community, they are not the elements which will galvanise society and thrust it towards new constitutional forms. We have now to look at Scotland's classes.

Scotland has a class system like all other Western countries. Our aristocrats have no influential rôle, having their centre of gravity fixed in London. There is a relatively small middle class and they live in areas of prosperity. In the Devolution Referendum of 1979, their business and commercial class interests quickly and comfortably identified with the "No" side. There were exceptions but by and large the private business sectors reacted in relation to their perceived interests. That does not make them traitors or quislings, or any of the other exotic names some nationalists throw at those who will not gallop down the independence road. It makes them normal. Since 1979, opinion, as measured by polls, has shown Scots once more back in the self-government groove. But, there has remained a consistent 25 per cent opposed to any change. Traditionalists in the SNP grieve over this, convinced that just a bit more preaching about national duty and insistence upon Scottish pride in the face of English contempt, will swing them over. Why should these people come over? They have been well rewarded for being British Scots. This minority can overcome its weak political position at Scottish elections by borrowing from the strength of Tory support in Southern England. The British-Scottish middle class can lose all the elections north of the border but still form the government in Edinburgh. Using that government, they can be appointed to the great network of quangos and so control Scottish policy and life. Their economic and political interests as a class are well catered for in the British context. When pressed hard in debate, they will not blurt out the truth about their vested interests. They will insist that they stand where they do because while proud to be Scots, they see themselves as British, a case of a belief arising from and then reinforcing a narrow interest. The middle class is not of course monolithic. The manufacturing interests within it have had their confidence shaken in the British connection by the consequences of Thatcher's policies and some thinking people in the financial institutions are worried by the lack of a political ring fence which would keep them safe from predators. Middle-class resistance to self-government is therefore weakening and is not something any of us should overlook. But the Scottish middle class will not provide the springboard for change.

It is to other interests and institutions in the community that the SNP must look for motives and needs which will propel events towards change. It so happens that the conjunction of institutional interests and patriotism is to be found among the working people. I am not abandoning, however, my main theme that vested interest matters above all when importing the notion of patriotic outlook. For years, while it saw its interests as best served by the British connection, the Scottish working class poured out its patriotism in a tartan exhibition along Wembley Way. But that ill-directed patriotism becomes important when the British connection ceases to be attractive. So a few moments thoughts on the working class and patriotism are called for.

Throughout history, and in many lands, while people from various classes have demonstrated a love of and willingness to sacrifice for the ideal of national freedom, it is the working people who provided the solid foundation for tenacious defence of that freedom. Working people have no wealth and, therefore, unlike others, do not look for bolt holes in which to place it when a country is under pressure. They are tied to their own country and so defend it. Had it been left to the common people and not the other interests subject to bribes, there would have been no Union of Scotland with England in 1707. To undo that union, we must now turn to the descendants of those common people.

The Scottish working class is not a group with a single all-embracing character. It is an amalgam of people who share a broad common identity born of history and contemporary circumstances, including the post-war growth of the public sector and the welfare state. They are profoundly anti-Tory in politics, firmly believing that intervention by government in economic policy is sound common sense and look to public sector activity and services to provide a good proportion of work and society's needs. Their vested interests are served by the institutions of the Scottish TUC, the education system, the health service, community groups and the Labour Party. They are not, as some Left romantics would have it, a hotbed of socialism. Scottish working-class development has been much influenced by socialist thinkers, ideas, preachers and events; this has placed them firmly on the Left of politics on the British spectrum. It is no accident that, whether it be miners or civil servants or teachers, Scottish trade unionists frequently demonstrate a more militant and radical attitude than their counterparts in England. But the working class does not see itself as an instrument for socialist advance. In many ways, the Scots are quite moderate in their economic demands and are socially conservative. Their militancy is roused by a sense of unfairness and their demands are for justice rather than a conscious overthrow of the capitalist system.

The Scottish working class are, however, a frustrated vested interest. Their sense of justice has been traduced by Thatcherism. The ideas absorbed from past socialist leaders have made them react to the New Right's vision of a society in which the strong prosper and the weak go to the wall. They are politically well organised, hold command of local government and in numerical terms are well represented at parliamentary level. Yet, the cohesion and political power which are their hallmarks have brought them no respite from the policies pursued by the Tory government, elected through English votes. In every direction in which its various parts turn, the Scottish working class faces the harsh truth that the constitutional status quo is a prison for its ambitions. No amount of renewed solidarity, increased industrial militancy, vigorous political campaigning or even support for their Labour Party will bring salvation. Who controls Scotland's working people is now decided in England.

The only way out is for the Scottish workers to turn towards self-government. That is the only direction in which their interests will be served. Their political institution, the Labour Party, is not capable of taking the lead. Labour as a party is terrified of the nationalist potential of the working people. Labour's function in Scotland is to damp down feelings and throw up obstacles and create diversions. Scottish Labour goes into a blue funk when posed the question of what they will do if the English put in yet another Tory government at the next election. Labour, as an institution serving the working class, is in an intrinsically weak position. Institutions must deliver, and if they cannot, become candidates for removal.

Provided it understands what is happening and can genuinely line itself up with the basic views and aspirations of the Scottish working people, the SNP can mobilise and lead this largest and most powerful vested interest in pursuit of independence within the European Community. The need of the working people and the logic of independence have, at an important historic time in the British Isles, become almost as one. To make them one, wholly understood as such by the working people, is the task facing the SNP. Succeed and we shall achieve independence. Success does not depend upon the SNP becoming a carbon copy of the Scottish end of the Labour Party, aping its antics and borrowing from its narrow vocabulary. SNP members are bound to react badly to any misguided attempt to force them into a Labour mould. They rightly see Labour as having failed Scotland. It was from the ranks of early Labour that the first modern cries for self-government arose. Yet, despite majority Labour governments armed with pledges to create assemblies, nothing has been delivered. Labour's electoral ascendancy since 1955 has been matched by Scotland's steady decline and rising poverty. Besides, to ape the Labour Party is no service to the Scottish working people. Between 1959 and 1964 the Labour Party in Scotland was dynamic and full of ideas about how to tackle industrial decline and conquer poverty for good. The failures of Wilson, Ross, Callaghan and Millan have eaten away its self-confidence. Now Labour makes a virtue of promising little. It is a negative force in Scottish politics, spending its energies against things, hoping that the noise created will deflect attention from the fact that it has nothing positive to say.

What is needed in Scotland is a New Left which is positive in outlook and modern in language. Which does seek to fire working-class imagination, stoke ambition and excite visions of a fair, just and healthy society — one where people can expand their personalities and breathe in an atmosphere that stimulates expansive thoughts and actions. What is needed is a party with ideas and drive, whose commitment is to create, for the first time, a Scotland that has its public policy shaped by the interests of the working people, shifting wealth and power to them. The Scottish working class, because their vested interests can only be met by fundamental constitutional change, represents the greatest force available to the national movement. But the working class has to be convinced that the kind of change advocated by the SNP will not deliver them into the trap of new centres and structures of power ending up in the hands of others.

A Scottish Parliament by itself is not a guarantor of working-class advancement. Who controls that Parliament and what instinctive philosophy will guide its politics are the key issues upon which working people judge the issue of self-government. Quite rightly, workers know full well that if the SNP takes Scotland to independence, then the SNP will form the early government of the new state. The party that achieves the breakthrough is almost certain to win the elections. Working people are thus inclined to judge the question of independence, as distinct from devolution, in terms of what kind of Scotland the SNP seeks to create. That is a perfectly legitimate test for the working people to set the nationalist party. When members of the SNP claim that any Scottish government of any political colour would not act against the interests of working people, they are not believed. Working people in Scotland have been as much, if not more, abused by fellow Scots than foreigners throughout the ages. Tartan Tories were never more benign than any other variety. In any case, it isn't simply a matter of not having a Parliament controlled by forces that would probably act against them. Working people want a Parliament that will work for them. A Parliament that will make the priorities for legislation and economic policies reflect the priorities of the working class.

Scotland's position economically and socially does not allow of policies that will placate every class and interest group. A full quarter of our population lives on supplementary benefit and one-third live in poverty. Twenty-five per cent of those in work earn less than £100 per week. Conditions in many areas where there is 100 per cent working-class housing are appalling. Oxfam gave money to Craigmillar housing area in Edinburgh and Christians in Kenya have made donations to relieve housing conditions in Edinburgh's Pilton area. Visiting European parliamentarians have been stunned by the housing and social conditions they found in the Glasgow peripheral housing estates. There are around 400,000 people unemployed in Scotland. To right those wrongs will demand the mobilisation of financial and physical resources, their allocation to programmes of reconstruction designed to lift working people from poverty and the improvement of their bargaining power with employers, thereby promoting new jobs and lowering unemployment.

This does not mean that a New Left SNP would or should seek to injure other sections of the Scottish community or go on a nationalisation rampage just for the ideological hell of it. We need entrepreneurial flair and ability to work in home and overseas markets and to carve out a Scottish share of new technology and associated research and development. These qualities do not naturally flow from public ministerial committees. Politicians and civil servants, however clever and able in their own fields, are not good at running businesses. They become hopelessly lost in the jungle of international competitive world markets. An eye for business and a zest to pursue new developments and market opportunities, together with the guts to take a risk, cannot be conjured up by legislation. Entrepreneurial thrust can be aided by public policies. This can be benefitted by funding designed to give access to business education, marketing assessments, deeper and wider links between business and the universities, as well as improved export aid.

But what the Scottish business community cannot have is a free hand on workers' wages and conditions; nor can it be allowed to avoid its share of financial responsibility towards the social framework. Business people are in business to make money. That is acknowledged. A mixed economy is a settled and accepted state of affairs to all but the ultra Left and extreme Right. But the experiment of reducing the rights of working people as a means of boosting business activity has caused untold misery; business had to be told bluntly that its continuation or repetition is unacceptable. Business in a New Left Scotland will have its rightful place in the scheme of things. It cannot, however, be allowed to dominate and determine the values by which all policy is influenced. Indeed, it must learn to live with a new set of values which give working-class interests and needs first priority. Where there is a fundamental clash of interests, those of the working people must prevail.

I have set out in this chapter to demonstrate that Scotland's institutions and vested interests are varied and, on certain crucial points, are at cross purposes: to chase the kind of national unity sought by the traditionalists is the naïve route to irrelevance. Reality in society is about the struggle for power and control of resources. Some Scottish institutions are blessed by the constitutional status quo and some cursed by it. Above all, I have tried to show that it is essential for a party seeking to lead a democratic revolution to ally itself with and become the accelerator of those interests and forces which must break the old system in order to survive and flourish.

The question for the SNP is whether it can cast off its old reluctance to admit reality and take sides within Scotland and do so openly in favour of working people, thus ultimately engaging their institutional power in the struggle for self-government. If it takes the plunge, the SNP will not find instant success. Working-class loyalty has to be won by consistent support for its causes. It will take time to establish the kind of instinctive trust that will permit the party to explain itself and be accepted.

The SNP has energy. The working class is a dormant power. Our task is to fuse our energy with that power. That is the way to achieve our kind of revolution.

G

*Chapter 9*

# THE NEW HERESY: A BELIEF IN FULL EMPLOYMENT

> Above all I curse and strive to combat
> The leper pearl of Capitalist culture
> Which only tarnishes what it cannot lend
> Its own superb lustre
> Somewhere in its creative faculty is concealed
> A flaw, a senseless and wanton quality
> That has no human answer
> An infernal void.
>
> Hugh MacDiarmid: *My Songs are Kandym*
> in *In the Wasteland*

THREE FAIRLY RECENT developments have combined to overwhelm many Western governments, destroy post-war certainties about sustaining full employment and grip people in a sense of despair. These are: substantial increase in oil prices from 1973 to the mid-1980s, the rapid spread of micro-chip technology and the rise to significant industrial power and competitiveness of a number of developing countries. An additional reason for concern in Western Europe in particular is the growing power of countries in the Pacific Basin. Some commentators claim this vast region is now becoming the dominant trading, industrial and technical area of the world. Indeed, the world's economic giant, the United States, is already accommodating to this by internal shifts of power, from the crumbling industrial base of the eastern seaboard to the western and south-western states, especially California. In

162

1983, for the first time, the United States trade with countries of the Pacific Basin exceeded trade with Western Europe.

All of these factors have perplexed European leaders, most of whose political and economic views were formed when European states dictated events over a large part of the globe: they now find it difficult to come to terms with the profound changes now underway. All of Western Europe's leaders were frightened by the possible consequences of massive unemployment. They prayed in aid the "international recession and crisis" and managed to create a belief among the peoples of Europe that "something" had gone generally wrong with Keynesian policy, thus producing acquiescence and not the anticipated social revolt. There have, therefore, been no irresistible pressures on these bewildered politicians and they have muddled along hoping that something would turn the world around in their favour once more.

In my view, the rising power of the Pacific Basin will not be arrested. It is part of the phenomenon of change in world economic power and influence. The challenge for Western Europe is to match the Pacific Basin countries in technical innovation, which requires a positive welcome and encouragement to new technologies and a desire to engage in research and development. The problem is that increased technical innovation, through the increased use of the micro-chip in productive and commercial enterprises, appears to threaten employment. I say appears because it could well prove that in the long run the technological revolution will create more jobs than it destroys. This is far from being proved, however, and what is known is that in the short run technical investment sheds jobs. As the short run can cover a few generations, the lives of many people will be adversely affected for a long time. I really doubt if "something" will just turn up for Western Europe. We shall have to achieve the rescue by ourselves.

At this stage, before we join the legion of leading politicians who claim a limited capacity to act and become equally overwhelmed by the feeling that nothing can be done, it seems wise to address first principles. I want to start at the human level. It is not my intention to explore matters on a purely philosophical plane. However, I do believe we should more frequently examine our fundamental values and attitudes to the development of human society before we go blithely into the realm of concrete policy-making or, in the case of employment, into a retreat.

I start, therefore, with the question: what is it that makes having a job important to the individual and how important is the kind of job he or she has? To understand the importance of having a job, it is first of all necessary to understand that while much has changed in the way of life of working people, especially over the past forty years, there is one enduring fact. The vast majority of people own no significant amount of capital and therefore have nothing to live by except selling their labour, whether it be manual or mental. Being able to sell your labour offers the chance of a good life but those unable to do so can hope for no more than subsistence living. Thus we see the vulnerability of most people in Western society and the social and economic importance of having a job.

There are elements in contemporary life intimately linked to a person holding down a good job. We live in a credit-based society. People in work not only have the security and hope that such a circumstance holds out but also find that credit doors become open, thus allowing enjoyment of a very wide social activity. There are, too, the building up of occupational pension rights, mortgages, and adequate family insurance cover: all of these are wholly dependent upon the employment status of individuals. There are many ramifications which flow from holding a job.

There is also the social importance of paid employment. It provides a feeling of independence and self-esteem: that independence may, if subjected to brutal analysis, be quite illusory because, in a changing society, people do lose their jobs. But the fact remains, that people with work are relaxed, enjoy a feeling of self-confidence and self-regard. There is some pride in earning their living — an echo of the work ethic. Crucially, there is a sense of self-control. People out of work are dependent on the state for income. They do not earn; they are given a handout — often in the most humiliating circumstances as anyone visiting a crowded DHSS office will witness. The facts that they are guilty of no crime and that they apply for subsistence benefit only because they cannot sell their labour in the market, do not lessen the pain or the sense of personal failure. The concept of the work ethic does lie deep: in so far as that ethic suggests that people should contribute to the economic life of society, no socialist can reject it, even although it was spawned in a non-socialist era.

It is true that today's unemployed can be defended against attacks on their integrity. Most decent people accept them as victims. But we cannot sit and whisper that telling truth into the ear of the unemployed person as he or she sits slumped in private despair, day in and day out. It is then that the unemployed, facing a future that offers nothing, become soaked in a sense of hopelessness with their dignity eroding and their personalities under severe strain. To the unemployed, each day does not bring a new challenge or even interest. Each new day is further proof of uselessness, of being surplus to requirements, of being a burden, of being trapped forever. The unemployed must anaesthetise ambition because to have it consistently and cruelly frustrated is too painful an experience to endure endlessly. If Western society does not act against unemployment, it is not only the victims who will suffer. The rest of us are affected one way or the other. For any society to function in a civilised way, not only is general consent to law and order required, but also, as a prerequisite to that consent, the feeling and belief on the part of every citizen that he or she is a valued part of the community. When people are excluded, as they are when unemployment stalks the land, the process of alienation is inevitable and there flows from that increased levels of tension and lawlessness, from which none can escape unscathed.

I have sought to demonstrate, briefly, the importance of people being in full-time work. Now I must turn to the other half of the question of principle — about how important is the kind of job a person has. Here we are linked immediately to the micro-chip revolution. In my view, this is a development that promises the chance of not only full employment but of employment that is fulfilling. But to harness the micro-chip to the service of human society and to ensure that its benefits are widely dispersed, we need to change basic attitudes so that the socialist ethic progressively replaces that of capitalism. I wrote earlier that it remains to be seen whether the new technologies will create, in net terms, more jobs. But this does not invalidate the prospect of full employment as the micro-chip enters more and more into our lives. What is welcome in the micro-chip is that it offers people the benefits of mass-production without the soul-destroying engagement of humans in dull repetitive operations. With the micro-chip, machines can do the work that machines are really for. Human beings can be set free to engage their creativity on work that they do well and in which they find satisfaction.

In present-day capitalist society, human beings are merely part of the total equation of production, distribution and exchange. When, like plant or machinery they become redundant, they go on the scrapheap. Of course, we do not physically crush and dump them, sometimes at sea, as we do old machinery or chemicals. We feed and water them at a minimum level but onto their own part of the total scrapyard they go. On television there have been documentaries showing the unemployed literally on the scrapheap, rooting around in the rubbish. That there has been no universal outcry is a mark of how far this society has slipped in its sense of collective morality. What socialists need to do is insist that we take human beings out of their rôle as a mere element in the capitalist equation and place them in the forefront of policy, with their needs, rights and obligations as the pre-eminent objectives to which all else is subordinated. That is actually a novel idea in most of Western Europe in 1986, although not in places like Austria and Sweden where policy is people-orientated. Until socialists challenge the capitalist view of people as cogs in the economic machine, we shall lose the argument to the Right. It is the capitalist system's downgrading and degrading view of human beings that is the flaw in its creative faculty and gives it a senseless and wanton quality.

Capitalism, as American society has proved, can produce a vast array of developments and incredible leaps in technical achievement. It can pour out a torrent of consumer goods that glitter and gleam attractively in well-designed shop windows. But it operates at a cost to humanity as anyone who has visited Harlem, the South Bronx and Skid Row in San Francisco will know. If people are a necessary part of the capitalist machine, they are taken care of — in the same way that other parts of the machine are well maintained. If they are not needed, they are rejected to rust and rot.

When I was on trial at Edinburgh Sheriff Court, along with Chris McLean, Dougie Robertson, Stevie Butler, Graeme Purves and Iain More, in October 1981, I had an interesting exchange with Sheriff Neil Macvicar. We had broken into the Scottish Assembly building on Calton Hill, in Edinburgh, to gain access to the debating chamber and there read out a statement protesting against rising unemployment. The Sheriff expressed some understanding of our concern, although in no way approving of our methods. At one point, when I was stating the opinion that unemployment was a crime, he interrupted to ask if I was seriously suggesting that it should be outlawed by statute. He was startled to receive an affirmative reply. Sheriff Macvicar, like the rest of society, had never contemplated an Act of Parliament laying responsibility on government to promote and protect full employment. No doubt most readers will share Sheriff Macvicar's puzzlement about how this could be done with any practical effect. I would urge *you* to pause and think. Our society lays statutory obligations on government, other bodies and citizens in pursuit of apparently difficult objectives, some of which are in the sphere of the mind. There is an obligation to supply clean water, to provide a proper education for children, to care for children to the point of taking them away from parents, to safeguard from infectious disease, to curb the harmful environmental effects of chemical processes and the nuclear industry and to behave with equity towards others of different races. Many are imperfectly executed but the constant whip of statutory requirement ensures that government and society bend their policy decisions in other fields to meet what are accepted as fundamental legal obligations in specified areas. Yet, on the most fundamental human right of all, that of having a job, there is no legal obligation. There should be.

An economic policy that had to attend to such an obligation would produce very different results from what we have come to experience in recent years. There is also the advantage in the change of climate and attitude that is wrought by statute. Governments and political parties do not live in a vacuum. They are responsive to social climate. The legislative prohibition on slavery and child labour did not end the practices overnight but it did help to alter the climate of opinion so that their practitioners could not sustain their rotten trade down through time. Once changed, the climate produces new varieties of thought and attitude. Today it would be impossible to contemplate slavery and child labour. Some day, it may be that future generations will find it incomprehensible that we have tolerated the punishing régime of unemployment.

Just how far away our society is from realising that full employment is achievable can be gauged from the speeches of Neil Kinnock, leader of the British Labour Party. In the *Sunday Mail* of 10th November 1985, he is reported as having attended a meeting of young people the day before. He was asked by them for a guarantee of a job if a Labour government came to office. He replied: "I am not going to tell people lies. Anybody who made such promises would be fantasising. They would be dishonest and show contempt for young people." Neil Kinnock thus confirmed his abandonment of full employment. Strangely, he did not see this as showing contempt for the young. He has swallowed the full draught of the poisonous conventional wisdom that nothing can be done about unemployment except, perhaps, to reduce it a little and wring one's hands in sympathy for those who cannot be brought into productive society. In that statement Neil Kinnock was not exhibiting commendable honesty. He was displaying weakness of intellect and a collapse of his socialist beliefs. Once a socialist, especially one who leads the British Labour Party, accepts the Tory contention that market forces determine the level of employment and that claims about the right to work are unrealistic, he is lost. The difference between him and the Tories is no longer one of dimension and values; it is merely one of degree measured by their values.

We are now confronted with what hitherto would have been unimaginable. Labour joining the Tories and Fleet Street, in supplying the people with a diet of economic lies! The political establishment, overwhelmed by the nature of the problem, unwilling to face the enormous task required for reconstruction and dogmatically opposed to a change in its ethical stance to put people first, opts for policies that will load the burden on the shoulders of a substantial permanently unemployed minority.

But because the leader of the Labour Party is bankrupt as a socialist, we here in Scotland do not have to follow his dismal lead. Unemployment has been no accident. It was in the July measures of 1975 (when Labour started to abandon its election manifesto of 1974), which deliberately created unemployment as a tool of economic management. Faced with the end result of their consciously chosen route (rising unemployment), Wilson and Callaghan tried to deflect criticism by praying in aid the so-called recession induced by oil price increases. Somehow, they managed to avoid explaining how it was that Britain, with North Sea oil bringing self-sufficiency, was in a mess, while Japan, with little or no energy resources, continued on a growth pattern.

Unemployment is deliberate. The policies that create it can be just as deliberately undone and replaced by those that will guarantee everyone a job. In today's Britain and Scotland that is heresy. If it were to be said in Austria, Switzerland, Norway or Sweden, it would be regarded as a perfectly sensible and workable proposition. They achieve very low levels of unemployment, not by accident, but by policy. Critics of these passages could say that all they represent are sentiments, not a practical base upon which full employment can be established. There is no intention in this chapter of evading *how* it can be done.

One more broad point is worth making before going into details of a solution within Scotland. It is concerned with the potential that now exists because of the release of human labour arising from the spread of micro-chip technology. Human beings not only represent a pool of physical power but are a reservoir of creativity and skill. Their release from humdrum tasks means that their vast talents are available for the improvement of society. It is people, not micro-chips, who are able to create splendour in our physical surroundings, to produce an upgraded environment that harmonises with our aesthetic values and to provide an intellectual atmosphere where thought once again becomes adventurous instead of backward.

The salient feature of Man is his creative faculty. People are our finest resource. We either throw them away, as is done now in capitalist society, or provide opportunities for them to flourish and have a dramatic and permanently beneficial impact upon society. The resolution of our problems is not to be found in the field of economics, however important that subject may be. Our salvation is to be found first in the realm of the intellect, in which imagination can make the quantum leap from despair to the seizure of opportunity. We have to replace the collective shrug of resignation, with a stirring of the mind and the human spirit.

But enough of these broad thoughts. Let us get down to hard cases, which apply these general principles (of people-orientation and the promotion of social and community values), to the specific situation of Scotland. What is set out below is a strategic programme for full employment, which can be achieved once we cast off the orthodox shackles of the Thatcher/Kinnock thinking — if such it be.

In Scotland the strategy must be to provide relief of the crisis by creating mass numbers of jobs in the short term, while simultaneously planning a permanent reconstruction of policy to operate in the long term. These are not separate, but complementary, elements in a single strategy. If people are not brought back into the world of work, and some introduced to it for the first time, we shall become progressively de-skilled and incapable of self-motivation. It is significant that the Roe-Erskine report on Bathgate in West Lothian, published in the autumn of 1985, identified a Third World dependence-syndrome in an area which has been pulverised by closures and mass unemployment. A society lacking in skills would render any long-term plan unworkable, no matter how good it was on paper.

The purpose of a short-term job creation programme is not only to give immediate relief to the unemployed. It is also to change the climate from one of fear to one of confidence. Confidence is a relaxant, giving people the capacity to make sophisticated value-judgements of how and when to adjust to changing conditions. Job protection through demarcation is not the action of the stupid or Luddite people: it is the response of frightened, insecure people. Therefore the objectives for the short term are to reproduce confidence, skills and open-minded adaptability. This can only be achieved in its first stages through public sector activity. Such is the scale of the problem that only the substantial thrust and co-ordination of the public sector will provide the basic answer. Although the public sector provides the financial resources and sets out the components of the programme, along with a fixing of time-scales, few elements of that sector will actually be engaged in the physical carrying out of the tasks. The private sector, and especially the manufacturers, will be the people doing contract work. They, too, will benefit from the change in climate and will have a basis of confidence upon which to plan for the future. By "public sector activity" I mean building and constructing things which improve both our economic potential and our environment.

We all know that further oil rigs will be required in the North Sea. Perhaps on this I am wrong, and that most people have bought the story that North Sea oil is over. It is a story that is being pushed quite hard, calculated to take the Scottish mind off the subject for good. The facts are different. When the history of the 1970s and 1980s comes to be written, historians will be puzzled by the oil phenomenon: how an intelligent, well-educated nation in a developed country became the only people ever to discover oil and get poorer. The oil issue in Scottish politics flared briefly in the early 1970s but since then, try as they will, the SNP have found it difficult to raise any interest. In the first decade of flow, £40 billion went to London's Treasury and in the second decade that will more than double to £90 billion. That such great capital resources should bypass the Scottish economy has raised no general anger or outrage. Oil should be central to the Scottish economic debate. It isn't even peripheral. It is a remarkable tribute to the manipulative skills of the English establishment that this should be the case. For generations it struck back at Scottish nationalism by claiming that the elements in the economic equation showed the result that Scotland was subsidised by England. We were too poor to become independent. Then came the oil: a new significant, overwhelming element in the equation, bound to produce a different answer on Scottish viability as an independent unit. This was dealt with by the simple expedient of removing oil revenues from calculations of Scottish GDP. Fish that are caught in the North Sea and landed in Shetland or Peterhead, or any other east coast port, count in our domestic statistics; the oil drawn from the same waters and landed in the same areas goes into a special non-Scottish account. Had the oil, like the fish, been put where it belongs, in Scotland's GDP figures, Scots would have been able to focus on a huge budget surplus which, properly used, could have saved us from the disasters of the past ten years. Who did the crooked accounting? It wasn't the English Tory government. It was a Labour government. Another Labour action for which Mrs Thatcher has been deeply grateful.

The fact is that between 1985 and 1995, there will be sixty-three new oil developments in the North Sea. There is also oil and gas in the Clyde. The North Sea Oil and Gas Spending Estimates (1985-95) show the staggering figure of £40 billion of equivalent orders within which are demands for production platforms, pipes and other steel-using items. A lot of this equipment can be built before time, put into a stock from which the oil companies are required to buy. That is what I am advocating as a prime public sector activity. I am also stating that, having got nothing of the £40 billion in the first ten years of oil revenues, the Scottish economy has a direct claim of at least 50 per cent on the £90 billion in this second decade 1985-1995. It is sound economic policy to build upon indigenous strengths. Oil is an indigenous resource of Scotland. It is only the poorest and weakest of Third World countries that are, wrongly, denied the ability to tap such resources and lay down conditions for equipment purposes. Right now the English establishment holds our people in thraldom with tales of Scottish dependency and inadequacy, while their hands are deep in our oil wells robbing us blind.

Any attempt to address the Scottish economic problem, without acknowledging the importance and promise that is inherent in the oil factor, is an act of dishonesty and stupidity. The Labour and Tory parties and the Scottish Liberals along with their allies have conspired to set aside all consideration of oil when contributing to public discussion in Scotland, although they all talk a great deal about it south of the border. For the nation to continue treading their false trail is madness. What would we all say of a man dying of thirst in the desert who, in finding himself at an oasis, refused to drink from the waters bubbling around him?

Public sector activity in other fields, such as building houses, schools, hospitals, roads and rail electrification projects, creates a demand for materials and creates work for people. Microchips don't swarm over a building site and, effortlessly as if by magic, produce a new hospital. It is the application of human effort and skill that does such things. Whether it be houses or hospitals, roads or rail, projects demand steel, concrete, cement, cables, electrical switchgear, pylons, scaffolding, wood, glass and vehicles to transport from manufacturer to site. In meeting the demand for materials, work is created in the manufacturing sector and other work is created in transport and construction.

This particular point about creating jobs through the public sector programme is nothing new, of course. Labour, Liberal and SDP are all in favour of something similar as a means of reducing unemployment. What their statements lack, however, is any sense of this short-term stimulus being part of longer-term strategy for recovery. The public knows that building a road, school or hospital will create work but they see little beyond that. After all, the road or whatever can only be built once; after it is done what then? There has been previously no convincing explanation. Indeed by proclaiming that they will only reduce not solve unemployment, the three parties mentioned above simply give credence to Mrs Thatcher's counterblast that these are not real jobs and not, therefore, the "real" solution.

It is only when the short-term programme is seen as a first step in a logical progression of rational planning and implementation that any belief can be expected to adhere: this sets the SNP apart on the issue of public sector programmes. It is an essential, but only a first step, to a more permanent situation where full employment becomes the norm. Lest the reader be misled. I should explain that "short term" does not mean a couple of years. The scale of reconstruction of our social assets, for example housing, is so great that it will require work for many years to come — and continuing maintenance and improvement. In November 1985, at a conference organised by the convention of Scottish Local Authorities (COSLA), delegates were informed that £3.5 billion needed to be spent on private and public sector housing if Scotland was to equal the standards in England and Wales. Mr Robert Lee, chairman of COSLA's housing committee, said:

> The government is too cowardly to allow a housing survey in Scotland because with the problems of dampness, asbestos, and tower blocks likely to fall down they are frightened that it would not allow them to ignore these problems any longer.
>
> (*The Guardian*, 30 November 1985)

The conference was told that in 1984 seventeen councils, including Glasgow and Edinburgh, built no houses at all and that 15,000 families a year applied for accommodation because they were homeless. Quite a message for St Andrew's Day!

What I see as the objectives of the short-term programme are these. First, to deal with the grave shortcomings in our economic and social infrastructure so that after about a seven-year period we emerge with a beautiful environment and superb services, together with a retooled and revitalised manufacturing sector. Second, to provide self-confidence to the people and create within their attitudes a training orientation.

While the short-term programme is underway, the planning and execution of the longer-term security of our economy gets full and parallel priority and direction. That means quite dramatic and fundamental change from present circumstances. *There is no possibility of designing and pursuing a long-term recovery strategy without self-government.* While we remain yoked to Whitehall, they will set the boundaries for our endeavours and these will be set narrowly. Just look at the long painful struggle of the Scottish Tourist Board for some minimal authority in its external activity! Battle after battle has been fought to remove obstacle after obstacle. That fight is as nothing compared to the resistance that Scotland would face, within the present unitary framework, if we sought to do our own thing in economic terms.

All our energies would be exhausted in the battle, which we could not win. Events have proved with different administrations that the Whitehall view will prevail because within the present system they exercise final control.

Look at the position now and in the recent past of the Scottish Development Agency (SDA). It has no independence. It is instructed by, and shackled to, the Scottish Office, which in turn fits neatly into its Whitehall rôle as a provincial outfit with a limited remit. The first priority now for those running the SDA is not to address the problems of the Scottish economy fearlessly and in forthright manner. The present chairman, in the first flush of his new office, did make one outspoken statement against government policy soon after the Tories came into office. He himself was their appointee. That didn't prevent Ministers and MPs from giving him a rough going over. In all the years since then, having been given the message, he and the Agency have behaved themselves. The Tories have no love for the SDA which was a Labour creation. But it would be politically difficult to demolish it entirely, so it has been allowed to survive in form as long as it does little of substance. Despite being the result of a Labour government measure, the SDA played a subservient rôle to the Wilson government's "national" body, the National Enterprise Board. It was well understood that the SDA played with the marbles while Whitehall's favourite body got on with the big stuff. In reality, the SDA could never fulfil Labour's 1974 pledge that it would produce a "Powerhouse Scotland". It has always been the means of camouflage — a front giving the impression of activity through reports and land reclamation, while the economy was being dismantled.

Only in a self-government setting can Scotland conceive its own economic strategy and pursue it without hindrance. It is in that setting, therefore, that my scheme for the long-term plan of recovery must develop. If there is no self-government, then certainly we can press for a modest public sector programme along the lines of Labour and Liberal ideas, but that will lead ultimately to nowhere.

Let us assume for the sake of argument that we in Scotland are finally in control of our own destiny and have the short-term programme underway. From Day One of that programme, in pursuit of the longer term, we shift the emphasis of the SDA from domestic to external activity. If we are to have a long-term future our manufacturing industry needs to have access to European and other foreign markets: before we can perform in these fields, we need to know what it is we must aim for. In other words, the future function of the SDA must be to answer the following questions:

1. What goods and services are going to be required in each of the world's main economic regions?

2. In which of these are there demands for products and services which can be met partly, or in whole, by Scotland's traditional technical and engineering industries?

3. Where, given that we are a small nation, are there demands for products and services that are imperfectly met but which could be met by new product development in Scotland?

4. What are the investment requirements, and the timing of investment, if Scottish industry is to make a successful penetration of the world's economic regional markets?

5. In which product areas should we be devoting our research and development effort?

That kind of work by the SDA would form the basis of an indicative economic plan upon which government and the business and financial institutions could found their activities. The SDA would accurately describe the targets and the investment and research means for producing a capability to hit them. Helping industry to hit the targets is a task for a specialist organisation. Gordon Wilson, chairman of the SNP, has advocated a Scottish Export Council. I have no quarrel with that excellent idea but believe that the Scottish Council for Development and Industry, an under-funded and underrated body these days, would perform that function. There is no point in creating new bodies when present ones, which have a fund of knowledge and ability, need only proper funding and a clear positive direction.

If Scottish industry is to make its permanent mark in the world markets, then it can only do so by the co-ordination of effort. We are a small country and few of our industries, if any, will have the independent resources necessary to carve out markets. Look at our smaller companies. How can we possibly expect them to take on the marketing giants of Japan and the United States? A small company faced with getting into, say, the Saudi Arabia market meets enormous problems well outwith the scope of its resources. It is through the formation of the Scottish Council for Development and Industry, as the country's export council, that co-ordination and penetration can be achieved. With the SDA constantly working on its external remit, and producing an indicative plan to which all can refer with confidence so that our export efforts are made in a coherent manner, we have the basic working model for long-term success.

But what about the people who work the model? Throughout this chapter, I have urged the importance of a people-orientated policy. No matter how good the theory or how attractive the model, nothing will work unless it harnesses the enthusiasm and commitment of the people. They have to see themselves as central to the whole system, as indeed they are. A long-term programme, unlike a short-term one, is no once-and-for-all measure. The long term will always be with us because it represents the challenge of an advancing future. It is the ability of people to adjust to change, to shed old skills and to take on new ones that is crucial to success or failure.

Training and retraining are the key. In the early stages of recovery it may be difficult to match training courses to specific job opportunities. In that situation, especially where we are dealing now with a couple of generations with no work or skill experience, it is important to see that training for its own sake has value. We have to give people skills upon which they can build other skills as time proceeds. It is always easier for skilled people, who approach problems in an analytical or experienced way, to learn new skills than it is for the unskilled. Training and retraining opportunities, throughout life, have to be seen as a right of the individual and an integral part of our whole economic and industrial effort. People in work should be positively encouraged to embrace new skills through training. People who, for whatever reason, find themselves out of work must have the right, and obligation, to engage in retraining.

Without wishing to weary the reader, I must repeat that our greatest resource is our people. Investment in their intellectual development, creating opportunities for human minds to spark and produce new ideas is of the utmost importance. Investment in their creative skills and ingenuity at the workshop level can only produce dividends. Encouraging people to take on a variety of skills increases the overall skill level in a society and enhances its adaptability. If Scotland is to compete and succeed in the world marketplace, it will be at the higher technical and engineering levels. We do not have a big enough home market to enter the mass production consumer goods stakes. It is in the areas of specialisation, where technical and design excellence hold the edge, that we must find our future. That is why the skill level of the people is so vital.

There is no magic required to create full employment within a nation of five million people which has such enormous resources of oil wealth and other inherent strengths such as the ability to feed itself from its agricultural base. We suffer from unemployment because the constitutional and economic machinery which govern us is misconceived. The post-war Scottish economy was flung together in an ad hoc fashion by the mandarins of Whitehall. We have been converted from a self-controlling to a branch factory economy — from relative strength to intrinsic weakness. As a result we could not stand against the recession brought in first by the Labour government and then intensified by Mrs Thatcher's government. The Scottish economy cannot support its people in work because it is under no direction, works to no strategy, has no coherence and is falling apart.

Direction, strategy, coherence are possible only when we exercise political control of our own nation and country. A Scottish Parliament will be a forum in which and through which we debate our future and our relations with the world outside. That is the only place where we can genuinely examine where we are, look at what we have, consider where we want to go and devise the means for getting there. Political control is a prerequisite of economic success.

Unemployment can be conquered. There is no need for Scots to listen any longer to the depressing defeatist wails of Neil Kinnock or wince under the grocer-shop nonsense that pours out of Mrs Thatcher. We have a choice. To remain as we are and go on as we are, downward. Or to take control and tackle the issue in our own way, on our own terms and in accordance with our own priorities. That is the only road to full employment.

*Chapter 10*

# SCOTLAND WITHIN EUROPE: THE FRAMEWORK FOR INDEPENDENCE

WITH THE SNP holding anchor position in Scottish opinion polls for the past three years, commentators outwith the country have believed nationalism to be on the wane. Their error arises from the mistaken view that nationalism cannot survive without the SNP. It is nearer the truth to assert that nationalism cannot manifest itself, or achieve its objectives, without a mature, self-confident and competent SNP providing direction and leadership. The same opinion polls that show a low rating for the SNP record 29 per cent of the people in favour of independence, with a large majority of the total population supporting a legislative Assembly with such economic and financial powers as to make it virtually autonomous within the UK. In 1979, in the immediate aftermath of the Devolution Referendum, Tom Nairn earned a great deal of scorn when he claimed that the events of that year, disastrous though they may seem, would not kill but stimulate Scottish nationalism. The polls are proving him right. The potential is there for all to see.

But it is no more than potential. Discussion and debate about what independence means in practical terms has been non-existent these past seven years. The debate will only come back with a return of SNP pressure with victories won in the ballot box. Then the unionist parties will try to squeeze the 29 per cent claiming to favour independence. Whatever their differences may be, the unionist parties will be as one in attacking "independence" as "separatism", with the latter deliberately ill-defined in order to promote as many nightmarish ideas as people's anxiety can invent. The old emotive words will spill from Labour, Tory and Alliance lips: "break up", "rupture", "dismemberment", "isolation". All drawn from the fear-mongering vocabulary of those who wish to stun the minds of the people, thus rendering them unreceptive to rational discourse. It is not enough, however, for nationalists to complain about the malpractices of their opponents. Despite having faced the difficulties that the "separatist" tag created between 1974 and 1979, the SNP has done little work on more closely defining what independence means in practical terms. They are thus too open for the crude but effective sloganising of the unionist parties. It is time for some fundamental thinking on the concept of independence, not only in the ranks of the SNP, but among Scotland's people in general. We in the SNP should start by accepting a truth. The doubts held by our group of potential independence voters, who go along part of the way but hesitate about the final irrevocable steps, are not without validity. Their collective caution will not vanish by increasing the volume of exhortation. They will only become convinced when the SNP faces up to certain economic and political imperatives which lie at the root of public doubt and anxiety.

In any attempt to achieve a sensible definition of independence it is clear that we must accept that certain factors and historic connections are vital. Geography, trade and industrial patterns, resources, cohesion, history and necessity all impose constraints on the exercise of sovereignty. In theory, every sovereign people can do what it likes. In practice, this is not so. And it is from the world of practice, in which we live, that we must draw on for our construction of a working definition.

No matter where one looks in the world, all countries have limits placed upon their sovereignty and independence by geopolitics or other factors, and the limits vary dependent upon the circumstances. Finland's independence is less than that of Sweden in relation to the Soviet Union, but greater than that of

Poland, which in turn is much greater than that of East Germany. Canada is better able to withstand United States pressure than is Mexico. Cuba proved more independent than Grenada. New Zealand is more resistant to United States military policy than is the larger country of the Philippines. Kampuchea is occupied by Vietnam, whereas the latter, as a close ally of the Soviet Union, suffers only border raids from China. The list of examples illustrates that it is a parcel of influences that determines how independent an independent country is. These examples point to the question: if independence cannot be exercised in full, why do so many countries and nations still cling tenaciously to the idea? Firstly, there is merit in almost every degree of economic and political independence that can be obtained and held. Secondly, the freedom of political action in countries, even where there exist severe externally based constraints, is a powerful medium of self-control, national identity, cultural vitality and a gateway to participation in the international community on an equal footing with many other peoples. There is another point. The surrender of sovereignty to international bodies and laws and the assumption of international obligations such as ILO conventions and GATT rules, is not regarded by independent countries as a shameful betrayal of their status. It is a series of obligations independently accepted in order that human society, on a world scale, can function with the minimum of friction and the maximum of harmony.

The reason for touching on other countries is not accidental. It is to emphasise that none, including Scotland, can avoid the limits placed upon their independence by certain factors, and the influence of those factors upon what the people may regard as the desirable form of independence.

Without doubt, the biggest influence on Scotland and her people has been the 270-year-old customs union with England which, together with the post-war centralisation of economic policy, has merged a great deal of Scottish economic activity with that of England. England takes about 80 per cent of our manufactured goods. Many of Scottish industry's marketing policies are obviously geared to English consumption. Scottish financial institutions have developed English markets. Insurance and pension fund investment has merged Scottish and English families in a socio-financial activity of a most important kind. Rolls Royce, Rosyth Dockyard, Yarrows, Babcock and Wilcox, Hoover and Ferranti are just a few companies with an integrated UK marketing and production policy. All underline the British connection that has developed as Scotland's branch factory economy has emerged over the past thirty years. We can deplore it, but we cannot ignore it. Certainly the people will not ignore it, they are in contact with the reality daily, as the lorries and trains with materials and finished goods pass up and down across the border and as the Scottish insurance companies gather in their harvest of English premiums.

For us, then, the essence of the independence issue lies in the customs union with England. Is the customs union to remain or go? That is the question. It cannot be dodged, because too many jobs, pensions and futures are tied up with it.

In my view, the only realistic reply is in the affirmative. for some, a continued customs union would be hard to stomach. A source of emotional pain. A reminder of England's historic dominant rôle in the British Isles. A frustrating continuing entanglement with the auld enemy from whom Scotland has never shaken free. In the face of such harrowing feelings, it is easy to dodge the issue of the customs union and opt instead for the platitudes about being part of the Commonwealth, or to invent the non-starter of Scotland in some Nordic tie-up with Scandinavia. Dodging the issue didn't work last time and will not work next time. If the SNP is to ensure that the next major constitutional debate about independence places them on the offensive and not defensively grappling with the jibe of separatism, the party will have to grasp the nettle. A continuing form of customs union with England is unavoidable. Acceptance of that reality will most definitely place constraints upon our independence. But the assertion of our acceptance of the customs union and our ability to place it cogently in the context of the wider European Community is the key to gaining independence.

Whether or not the SNP can place the debate about Scotland's constitutional future and relations with England in the wider context of the European Community is crucial. To allow the debate to develop as though it was merely an affair between nations on the island of Britain is the road to defeat because it is unreal. Along with many others, I campaigned against entry to the EEC, and many feel that our judgement has been vindicated by events. When the people voted to remain in, through a referendum in which the Scottish vote was noted separately, then a page in history turned in such a way that nothing of the past can be recaptured. Since 1972, and especially after the referendum of 1975, we have been set on a course of intimate involvement with other members of the Community. The Community dimension in our political, economic and constitutional lives has grown and will continue to grow. Scotland is now as much a part of the European Community as she is a part of the United Kingdom. Local authorities now beat a path to Brussels, as well as to Edinburgh and London. The European Social Fund, the Regional Fund, Common Fisheries Policy, the Common Agricultural Policy and the power of the Coal and Steel community are weaving their way into our lives. The frequent summits, the regular meetings of the Council of Ministers, the enhanced prominence of the European Parliament and the increased domestic reportage of them, all illustrate just how far the process of involvement has gone.

When one repeats the question about the customs union in the context of the European Community, then it becomes quite awesome. The reality is no longer an arrangement between Scotland and England. The customs union is now Europe-wide, embracing twelve states with a total population of around 270 million people. For the SNP to say we are not set upon maintaining our position within the customs union, leaves us open to the charge of double-separation: "Peeling off from England and the EEC", as our opponents will have it!

If, however, the SNP makes its target independence within the European Community and does so without ambiguity, then it is we who are backed by the solid advantages of political and economic logic, and the unionists who are left flat-footed. With an independent Scotland within the Community, the charge of separatism disappears. By definition, one nation or state cannot be separate from others while being a partner in a customs union. Moreover, the Treaty of Rome guarantees that there could be no financial, commercial or trading discrimination against a Scottish government and its people in any part of the Community. Continuity and lack of disruption becomes the key factor in this policy. There will be no change in trading relations with England or any other Community country as a consequence of Scottish independence: no change in social relations, continued freedom of travel and living in different parts of the Community and continuity of market access for industrial products. Scottish companies and those firms which have settled here in order to gain access to Europe can maintain their strategy without fear. Anxiety about job security among workers with markets in England and Europe would be fully met. Whether at the commercial or personal level, the British connection which is both practically and psychologically important to the Scots is maintained. The separatist gibe is silenced. What *does* change is Scotland's political position and influence, not only over those domestic affairs that are outwith Community control, but within the policy-making bodies of the Community itself. Scotland loses nothing in its trading access, but gains considerably in its elevation as a distinctive European political entity.

At present there is a number of small nation states within the Community. Compare them with Scotland:

| | |
|---|---|
| Scotland | 5,200,000 population |
| Luxembourg | 375,000 population |
| Eire | 2,800,000 population |

| Denmark | 5,000,000 population |
| Belgium | 9,600,000 population |
| Netherlands | 13,700,000 population |

Each of these small nations does better than Scotland in terms of ensuring that its unique position is taken account of when Community policy is decided. They have a direct say and vote at the Council of Ministers. They take their turn to chair the Council. They appoint their commissioners and they have their share of Community civil servants who, because of the important rôle of the Commission in drafting policy initiatives, are extremely important in ensuring that all member states' positions are taken into account. The independent status of Luxembourg and the others puts them into a different class of representation to us in the councils of the Community and gives an influence on policy from the very start of its formulation. Take two important examples. Scotland contributes most to Common Market fish stocks and oil from Scottish waters will figure largely in any attempt to create a common energy policy. Yet Luxembourg, with a smaller population than Edinburgh, and without either a coastline or an oilfield, will have a greater say on these vital Scottish interests than the Scottish people.

The advantages of independence within the European Community were spelled out very clearly by Senator Michael Yeats, at a conference in Edinburgh on Thursday, 29 December 1977. He was a vice-president of the European Parliament and leader of Ireland's Fianna Fail delegation. He pointed to Ireland being the second smallest state, yet claimed that its influence abroad was now greater than at any time in the past fifty years. Economically the Irish had been dominated by the outside world and by the United Kingdom in particular. In trade negotiations between the two countries, both sides knew that whatever the UK government decided to give was what the Irish were going to get.

> But at Community level we have an equal voice with the British government, or any other government for that matter.

He pointed out that dependence on trade with Britain had diminished from 75 per cent before entry to 47 per cent by 1977. On Scotland his view was:

> Scotland, as with Ireland, would find its interests being treated more seriously than in the past. At the moment they are completely dictated by whatever policies are laid down in London. On social and economic issues the extent to which they consider Scottish interests is up to them.

That speech was reported on 30 December in *The Scotsman*: too near Hogmanay for a nation, about to celebrate with its traditional binge, to take much notice.

The fact is that Scottish and English interests in policy often conflict and what is a priority or national interest issue in Scotland is a peripheral one in UK terms. In coal, oil, steel, transport, fishing and regional economic development, Scottish policy would differ markedly from that of England. Scottish coal, steel and fishing are peripheral in the context of the United Kingdom, as are transport and economic development of our island communities. There is no prospect of the UK government allowing Scottish need to impinge upon policies which, of necessity, it must pursue for the main component of political Britain — England.

As the European Community develops and extends its influence on policy, it is essential that Scotland has a seat at its top table where issues are considered and policy decisions made. Our physical geography places us on the edge of Europe, but by an exercise of will we can place ourselves at its political heart. As the oil-rich nation of the Community, prepared to contribute in constructive fashion to its development, we would indeed, in the words of the Irish Senator Yeats, have an "influence well beyond" our actual size. This policy is the antithesis of separation. There is nothing narrow or chauvinistic in its sweep. It seeks partnership on an equal footing with other peoples in the Community — a partnership where we willingly merge our sovereignty with others, and in which we play a full part in the evolution of Western Europe.

There are of course people in the SNP of very broad mind and with an internationalist outlook who will find it difficult to accept this policy. They look with horror on the centralist forces at work within the Community, the desire for political union on a federalist basis which would ultimately lead to a common and enforceable Community defence policy. Their anxieties are not without foundation and are shared by me and many others in the party. However, I come back to a point made earlier about the limits to independence set by factors of trade, industry, history and necessity and how these are perceived by and in turn influence the people.

The brutal truth is that Scotland's people have no modern tradition of independent action which would convince them of a policy of going it alone. More than most, they require firm ground to be laid out before they feel able to step upon it. They have too many irons in the British and European fire to pull them out altogether and at once. It is cruel, but true, that Scotland is a branch-factory economy and such an economy geared to a European/English market has no *early* wide options. Geopolitics, industrial orientation and history bind us to the European Community. It is a futile, senseless waste of Scottish political energy to seek our independence outwith the Community.

Our task in the SNP is not to salve our own conscience or tailor policy to the world that we would like to live in. Right now, our country is prostrate. It has no power or influence. We are a small country but of strategic importance to our European neighbours and to the superpower of the United States. It is naïve in the extreme to believe that we would be allowed to go our own way without other powers using our trading reliance on Europe/England to threaten openly the separatism we are so anxious to avoid and which would frighten our people into submission to the status quo.

The European Community is here to stay but it will not stay as it is. The Community has gone through three distinct phases: its establishment by the original six members, its enlargement to nine when the UK, Eire and Denmark joined and its further enlargement to twelve members with first Greece and then Spain and Portugal. It has become bigger, looser and has lost its sense of direction. Indeed, it often appears paralysed. But a Community of some 270 million people with many talents will not remain paralysed for ever. Efforts are underway now, through the Spinelli and Dooge reports, to break the constitutional chains on forward movement. These reports confirm the centralist tendencies within the Community's institutions and press for advance towards political union on a federalist basis. That is the wrong direction for Europe to travel in but these centralist forces will edge forward unless those of us with a different view of European development take an active rôle in the debate. The Community will change. The question is: who will make the changes? If we stand back, it certainly won't be us. It is of first-class importance that the Scots, via their own government, contribute directly to the discussions and take part in the formulation of new structures and policies. Indeed, the achievement of Scottish independence within the community would be a great reversal of centralisation and force the peoples of Europe to look afresh at the way the pursuit of centralisation has created impasse.

For the reasons set out in this chapter, I believe there is solid strategic and tactical value for the SNP in making a candid statement of policy to the effect that our advocacy of independence is defined within the permanent framework of the European Community. We need a bold statement of cardinal principle that places us firmly in the new reality of the Community. Happily the SNP's need and Scotland's conjoin. To survive and flourish as an economic entity in a grouping that now stretches from Shetland to the Greek islands, Scotland must be at the centre of decision-making. That can only be accomplished by the achievement of independence within the Community.

But it is not for tactical advantage alone that such a policy is advocated. The present paralysis of the Community is a matter for deep concern. If it is not solved, then the economic and social crisis which afflicts every nation will not be lifted easily. Millions of European citizens, especially the young, will stand condemned to a life of material poverty and unfulfilled potential. Europe will become a less civilised place as the decline gathers pace. This cannot be allowed to happen. It would be arrant nonsense to suggest that merely by Scotland gaining independence and member-state status, the Community would be energised and refreshed. But Scotland taking such a step would mean that we Scots had the opportunity to participate in the debate about how to move forward. That is important for us. Our presence would also demonstrate that the Community was not frozen but could be sensitive, responsive, capable of releasing the energy and enthusiasm of one of its many nations. If it could be done with one, then perhaps it might reach out to all the other peoples.

Scots are so used to being in a provincial backwater that we shy clear of making claims about our potential impact upon the wider human scene. But it is time to set aside this self-effacement.

We can make a significant contribution to the development of European institutions, because we know from experience what it is like to be on the receiving end of policies on which we have had no more than peripheral influence.

We can reinforce the cause of the small nations and the autonomous groups inside Europe and start a movement designed to force the institutions to be more open and receptive, recognising the legitimacy of the decentralist case.

There is a lack of leadership among Europe's small nations. Too often they readily allow the larger units to dictate the agenda and point the direction for future development.

I see a leadership rôle for Scotland within the Community, leading the coalition of the small against the large, and winning.